The Priests We Need
to Save the Church

Kevin Wells

The Priests We Need to Save the Church

SOPHIA INSTITUTE PRESS
Manchester, New Hampshire

Sophia Institute Press
Box 5284, Manchester, NH 03108
1-800-888-9344

www.SophiaInstitute.com

Sophia Institute Press® is a registered trademark of Sophia Institute.

Library of Congress Cataloging-in-Publication Data

Names: Wells, Kevin (Kevin J.), author.
Title: The priests we need to save the church / Kevin Wells.
Description: Manchester, New Hampshire : Sophia Institute Press, 2019. | Summary: "This book delineates the skills and virtues Catholic priests need today in order to lead to heaven those persons under their care"— Provided by publisher.
Identifiers: LCCN 2019028110 | ISBN 9781644130322 (paperback)
Subjects: LCSH: Priests. | Pastoral theology—Catholic Church. | Proselytizing.
Classification: LCC BX1913 .W436 2019 | DDC 262/.142—dc23
LC record available at https://lccn.loc.gov/2019028110

For Joe Patanella,
who showed what a father does, until the very end.

"I will give you shepherds after my own heart,
and they shall feed you on knowledge
and sound teaching."
—Jeremiah 3:15

Contents

Prologue

I squinted into the sunshine and saw him standing there, looking at me, smiling, from his shoebox-size rectory deck. It was June 6, 2000, as important a day as I'll ever have. I stepped out of my car and realized he had already fallen into that radiant, mocking manner of his that I had seen countless times over the years: hands on hips, slowly shaking his head as if he had caught me eating a third powdered donut. Those blue Irish eyes, which spoke paragraphs before he ever opened his mouth, looked into mine. They spoke lamentation this early evening. They cut right through me. "I know it's crushing you, Keggy. It's hell," they seemed to say. "But come."

He turned his eyes to the broken flower beside me, Krista, my wife. He seldom looked my way again. We walked up the narrow, wooden deck steps and into the booming presence of this rare priest, my Uncle Tommy, Msgr. Thomas Wells.

Krista and I couldn't bear children. Our recent honeymoon prayer in the Tuscan countryside was for ten. So the news of our infertility felt like the thin, plunging blade of a guillotine. At the top of the steps, Tommy, as our family affectionately called him, flung out his long arms and waited for Krista to walk into them. He didn't presume a warm hug, and he didn't get one.

Her sorrow had become suffocating. Tommy knew my wife was determined to fight for the child whom doctors promised could grow within her. His brief, knowing look to me said, "Hey, Keggy, do your best just to clamp it tonight. Okay, bud?"

I had called him from D.C. Beltway traffic earlier in the day, a call I had avoided since Krista and I had left our settled lives in Florida for Maryland after discovering our infertility. Ever since winter, I had kept Krista far away from him because of her eagerness to pursue pregnancy through in vitro fertilization, an intervention I rejected. With his steadfast adherence to the principles of natural moral law and Catholic teaching, I knew Tommy would agree with me. It would be two against one, but Krista didn't care.

Our discussions on the ethics and morality of building our family through artificial means of fertilization had devolved from measured dialogue to argument, then to feud. I had fallen into a new pastime, during noiseless drives home from work, of mentally framing positive justifications for adoption. At home, I'd delicately unpack and propose my thoughts to Krista, who would handily reject them. Coldness had settled in between us, pushing us into a soul-wrecking place of insolubility. She returned to calm only when I walked into another room. We walked around our small apartment like ticked-off zombies. The tension felt like an oppression, and soon it seemed as if demons were circling above like vultures surveying the potential for marital roadkill.

"Tommy, we're broken in half," I admitted on the phone, looking up into the sky-swallowing Mormon temple off the D.C. Beltway. "Krista cries herself to sleep. And I can't comfort her."

"Buddy, come over," he had said. "Bring Krista."

After Tommy broke from Krista's limp hug, he pulled out a few plaid deck chairs, opened a bottle of inexpensive red wine, and sat across from us, a still, calming center to our fractiousness. The colors of the summer sky were just beginning to deepen. He looked at me quickly, then turned his focus and attention to Krista and clucked his tongue—*tsk, tsk, tsk, tsk*—in that way of his. He studied her hazel eyes and shook his head slowly, a movement that looked like "no" but actually meant "yes, I get it." He curled his tongue into a corner of his mouth and focused on her face. He kept still in what seemed a genuflection to Krista's brokenness. Then he smiled. When he finally spoke, he sprang: "It's God-awful Krista. It is awful."

Krista's icy facade broke, and tears came at once. And Tommy's eyes went watery, though he kept smiling.

He seemed to know something we didn't and kept shaking his head. Then he turned our world upside down.

"You two have no idea how lucky you are," he proposed, glassy-eyed, smiling. "You've got no idea, do you? He picked you two, you see. Jesus gave you His cross. He's asking you guys to carry it with Him."

In just a sentence or two, he brought us to Golgotha, to the foot of the cross, where for the first time in months, a pinhole of illuminative light shone through. Tommy's words could have seemed ridiculous, cruel even, but the surge of warmth we felt told us there was order in them. He sensed a sudden opening in our wound, so he stepped further into it, enlightening us on the inside-out, illogical way of God's love.

For months, we had found our cross of infertility revolting and unbearable, a blanket of thorns. Tommy insisted on telling us that what we regarded as a diminishment was actually pure gift. "Of course it's miserable. I know it is," he said, leaning toward us. "But you gotta see this, guys—there's so much goodness in it."

No question that it was a whale-sized cross, he agreed. Nobody would want it. Regardless, he suggested that we try to view it as a crucifixion to embrace.

"This thing you guys have," he said, thrusting his hands forward as if wanting to dump the idea into our heads, "is a sign that God loves you uniquely, you see."

Our eyes narrowed, especially mine; I was the one with the low sperm count. Sensing our unwillingness to "embrace crucifixion," he started delicately unpacking the mystery of the cross. He had already managed to direct the flow of the conversation — there was no easing into it with discussions of the weather, work, or the ride over to his parish church, Mother Seton. We opened ourselves up to his plunging, intense manner because we knew he had invited us over to keep us from drowning; this was a rescue mission. And really, we didn't mind listening to someone else's voice for a change. That alone seemed a balm for wide-open sores. So, he dug up relics of Catholic thought on redemptive suffering.

Uncle Tommy explained that bearing our cross was both a point of departure and a shortcut to freedom. "Jesus came to save us. But if you think about it, He really just came to save us from ourselves," he said. A life of sanctity, he explained, almost as if he were breaking down a mathematical formula to its simplest form, never really begins until the work of renouncing oneself begins. Most people never get this, he said. "Naturally, people want pleasure and will do everything possible to avoid pain. But most will never understand the depth of peace that comes from taking on a cross they didn't want." This action of self-denial, of taking the narrow way, he said, was the perfect prayer, because it unites us perfectly to God's will. It was as if Tommy was lifting the latch of a swinging gate for us to pass through so we could hand everything over to God.

Then he brought us deeper, as if leading us into a cave. His exuberance and love were torchlight for us, so we trusted his lead. It was *our* cave, in fact, the darkness we both felt. But he explained that order and harmony could be found in total darkness by resigning ourselves completely to God's providence and will for us. He said that the saints became heroic by working in total darkness. I had spent many hours with Tommy over the course of my life, vacationing with him in Ireland, Montana, the Berkshire Mountains, on shorelines, and numerous other places unremembered. His power, I knew, sprang from his gut, his reason, and an attentive, joy-filled heart. He had straightforward opinions and a zeal for untangling problems by rolling out the cashmere blanket of Catholic truths. This storehouse of dogma and doctrine, sanctified by time and lived out by saints, sparked the countless leaps he had taken into souls down the years.

Tommy proposed that even within God's mysterious plan for our marriage, and its seemingly permanent childlessness, we should bend our will entirely to His—no matter how disregarded our action seemed. This was the mystery of the cross. Christ's love subsumed all heartbreak, rage, and desolation—and *gave it inexorable purpose*. Walling ourselves off in a catacomb of self-pity served no purpose, and it would cave in on us eventually anyway. Tommy encouraged us to set blister-shouldered Simon free to beat the long path back to Cyrene. It was our time now to bear the full weight of the cross, our opportunity to resign ourselves to God's mysterious plan. He didn't soften the ground for us; He asked that we walk it like saints.

Then Tommy said the unsayable: infertility was the complete measure of God's love poured into us. Our eyes stayed in a squint. He explained that it was Jesus' invitation to know Him fully. Tommy was trying to tell us that the deepest lash of the soldier's whipcord could be partly ours now, a scar that would forever speak to us of our need for supernatural faith and total abandonment to God's will. The embedded thorns, the Garden desolation, the friendlessness — it was ours for the taking to be by Jesus' side — if we just bent our wills some. Just as Christ's Crucifixion marked the fullest measure of His love spilled out for the world, Tommy said, the cross of our infertility was the apogee of His love for us in particular. We weren't following. Our screaming matches didn't feel like God's stamped approval of love. The paradox needed untangling, so Tommy leaned forward, his long arms waving.

"He wants you in the fight with Him, don't you see? All of this pain you've been feeling is for your sanctification," he said. "Maybe it's for someone else, but I don't think so. I do know it's God's way. No matter who benefits," he continued, "your surrender to God's providence will change you forever. Trust Him with it."

Our cynicism was starting to break apart, to lift and slip into the summer sky. Tommy's every gesture, word, and teaching seemed to urge, "Come, Keggy, come, Krista — see. See it!"

He said that God had a special way of handling these types of agony. We'd see a cross, but He'd see a *fiat* — "let it be done to me." We'd see forsakenness that bit into our souls, but He'd see an opportunity to build trust. We'd see desperation, but He'd see an opening for us to surrender to His way. We just needed to embrace the painful, silent groan now. A patient acceptance of God's strange purpose in the lonely realm of our infertility would bring peace and enormous reward. Tommy guaranteed it, and his toothy smile grew as wide as I had ever seen it.

But just as quickly, he let it go.

Tommy had saved the worst for last — but he was a man, so he said it. He looked to Krista, inhaled deeply, slowly shook his head, and clucked his tongue again. He said that starting a family through the tempting science of in vitro fertilization would be like answering yes to the ancient serpent: "Let me become like God." "Krista, I don't know why, but God willed this thing to be," he said. "I beg you, try to take on the attitude of the cross, not the attitude of the world. I beg you. At the very least, pray hard on it."

Krista said very little throughout the evening. Her tears spoke for her. And she said nothing to his final plea because she was weeping. Before our departure, on our walk to the car, Tommy stopped and hugged tired Krista beneath the night's first stars. "I'll be there for you," he said, "throughout it all."

The gate was wide open now. I guess we walked through — but I was holding my breath and didn't notice.

The hour-long car ride home was silent except for the sounds that accompany tears. He had cracked us wide open. Krista stared out the window, mourning, I imagine, children she longed for but her womb would never carry. Before collapsing into bed, for the first time in weeks, we fell into a long, quiet embrace. Looking back, I imagine I had never loved Krista more than I had that day.

The next morning, I awoke before dawn in nervous anticipation, wondering if we had actually passed through that gate; were we in a different place now, finally? I reached for my rosary and watched daylight filter into our small family room as a seemingly benevolent mist. A few songbirds, not vultures, bounced from branch to branch in the oak tree outside. The shock of what had unfolded the night before transformed what had been a teeming jungle into what seemed a new countryside of consciousness and settled peace. For the first time in many months, I was hopeful of a unified path, but I wouldn't know fully until Krista looked me in the eye and said so.

The Priests We Need to Save the Church

It wouldn't be a typical day—not only because of our previous evening, but because I was scheduled to undergo a fourth arthroscopic surgery on my right knee. Just another uncooperative body part. Krista slept. I can't remember if I was chewing my fingernails or not, but I knew I'd stay quiet about the previous night until Krista spoke up about what seemed in retrospect a staggering Catholic omnibus on self-abandonment and the cross.

We were in the hospital waiting room when Krista finally spoke. She told me that Tommy's words made sense and that the pathway he had laid out seemed right, though its route for us seemed lonesome and merciless. She thought she could grow into the idea of putting her trust in God and walking away from in vitro fertilization. In other words, Krista had just nailed her will to the cross.

"I was furious with God, with you, and with the way everything had turned out," she confessed. "But last night and all this morning, I do feel at peace, Kevin. I do. I think I can do this, or I'm gonna try."

At that moment, the surgeon could have sawed my leg off, and I'd have tipped him 20 percent.

Picture yourself in a pit core-drilled far down into the bottomless darkness of the earth. No one knows you're there. There's no way out. And there are teams of demons down there with you. Then a flashlight shines, and a voice calls out from very far away, from above: "I'm here."

That's what it felt like—what my uncle, Msgr. Thomas Wells, did to pull me and Krista out of the hell our lives had become. We each needed wrenching, even dragging, but shepherds—the true ones anyway—are guardians of souls. They deliberately push through their sheep's horror, wrongheadedness, and dark forests of grief to staunch wounds, renovate souls, and turn things inside out. We limped into Tommy's presence as scarecrows left to disintegrate in a forgotten winter cornfield, and we came home with poetry set into our souls.

My uncle's single-minded intention was to rely on unchangeable and reasoned Catholic principles to break through the barrier the pastor at our seaside parish in Florida had unwittingly erected. That priest had told Krista, his youth minister at the time, that in vitro fertilization was permissible if our consciences were "clear and settled." He knew that Krista had a mother-bear ferocity to have children, and he gave his blessing to pursue that desire with a procedure that Catholic teaching clearly forbids. I suppose he imagined he was doing us a favor by granting us permission to reconfigure teaching and thus allow our tired souls to achieve what they longed for. But looking back, I saw that his words contaminated our young marriage by causing a canyon to form between us. Ironically, his compassion stripped and deprived us of the very thing that that priest was ordained to impart to us — intimacy with the cross and the agony of Christ. Although desperate and wounded at the time, what we needed was an eternal perspective based on Catholic doctrine, regardless of how it "tasted" to us. We suffered the pain of infertility. But our entire married life went into free fall and was led into a spiritual wasteland because of the lie that priest had introduced into it.

Tommy was a counterrevolutionary toward the ideas of modern Catholic thought, the antithesis of priests such as the one who failed us. I imagine he would have liked to have thrown that priest (and doctrine-twisting priests like him) off the Sunshine-Skyway Bridge, just to awaken him to the aggravation and the distortion he had caused in us and perhaps in other souls in travail — in the name of pastoral sensitivity and accompaniment. He wouldn't have dared whisper it, but Tommy knew that that priest's permissive imprimatur could have eventually led to the damnation of our souls.

The surgeon cleaned out my knee again and sent me home later that day. If I elevated my leg for two days, I could then return to work on crutches. On the drive home, Krista told me she had begun researching adoption agencies while I was in surgery. God had taken away. Perhaps God would also give.

The next morning, Krista left for her work at a local bank. Mom came over a little later to make breakfast, because my doctor's orders were to stay in bed. I couldn't wait to tell her the news of Tommy's words and of Krista's change of heart. For Mom, the most faithful woman I knew, the news couldn't have been better if Gabriel had brought it himself. She had been offering Rosary after Rosary for us.

But not long after I had shared the heartening news, our home phone rang. Mom answered for me. It was Dad.

She fell to the ground. Over and over she screamed the same three words.

No. Not Tommy.

No. Not Tommy.

Plunging into anguish, she curled herself into a fetal position and writhed, as if she'd been shot in the stomach. Mom, the humblest, most unobtrusive person I knew, was doubled over in wild-sounding sobs. Everything assumed a slow-motion preternaturalness. I rolled off the bed and moved to try to comfort her, but I didn't yet know what had happened. Nothing was normal—the awkward fashion in which I held Mom, her heartrending screams—the bizarre news she told me. Someone had murdered Uncle Tommy. He had been stabbed to death in his rectory.

Eventually Mom rose from the floor and told me to call Krista. Her throat was raw. She staggered out the door to be with Dad,

Tommy's older brother, who was racing to meet her. I lay on the carpet, my mind a wildfire. Poor Krista came home wide-eyed. "Turn on the radio," she said. "The news is everywhere." My wife's new spiritual shepherd lay dead in that same rectory, knife wounds marking the length of his body and face like stigmata from hell.

Reporters rolled like thunder into quiet Germantown, Maryland, and detailed the gruesomeness of the murder. A man with a knife had broken into Tommy's rectory in the middle of the night. When Tommy didn't show up to celebrate Mass in the morning, a church employee walked over to the rectory and into the crime scene. We learned later from detectives that a homeless drifter—Robert Paul Lucas—had stumbled out of a local bar, high on cocaine and alcohol. He wedged himself through an open window into the rectory and stabbed my uncle dozens of times. Lucas claimed that he was trying to clean up after urinating on himself. When he stepped from the rectory in blood-stained boots; he didn't consider the tracks that would eventually betray him.

At daybreak, hours after Lucas's inexplicable deed, an immense shifting shadow seemed to have fallen upon a portion of the eastern seaboard of America.

"Lucas was a weak man—but it was among the most brutal and violent murder scenes I've been involved with," said Deputy State Attorney Kay Winfree. "I always thought there was something in Lucas's past that led him to act with that magnitude of violence. . . . I don't know—maybe he was once abused by a member of the clergy."

1

An Ax, a Tomahawk, and the Night of Lights

Eight years after the violence visited upon Tommy, I asked God for some of my own. I didn't need Him merely sharpening me or firming me up. Specifically, one night in December at around midnight, I requested his ax at the root. The moment the request left my mouth, it seemed like a drunken dare, but I didn't take it back. I just kept repeating it.

It was on the eve of the last day of a long weekend of meditative prayer, during which, one by one, my sins, failings, and omissions had washed like sludgy red tidewater into my conscience. I dropped to my knees on a graying, gap-tooth-planked dock on the banks of the Potomac River, mere steps from where John Wilkes Booth had hidden on the night he gunned Abraham Lincoln down. Gusts whipped up small waves on this wintry night, and a countryside blanket of stars and a nearly full moon cast what seemed like floods of Bethlehem light on the brutality of my request. Tears eventually came, because I felt I had passed into a wild land of consequence, where God would grant my request.

Wise parents had taught my seven siblings and me that God didn't waste these types of prayers.

I had returned this weekend for yet another men's silent retreat at one of America's quaintest prayer hideaways, a large aging brick structure that rested like a cheerful postcard of harmony beside a sheer cliffside, overlooking a wide expanse of the Potomac. Same cold weekend as many times before. Same pleasant Jesuits. Same contemplative retreat structure. Same tender silence with Christ. Perhaps because I had just turned forty, this weekend turned uncharacteristically solemn and introspective soon after I had dropped my bag off in my room. Thus began a self-analysis, tracing the development of my life since the time I first attended the weekend retreat two decades earlier as a college student.

As the weekend progressed, self-awareness began to poke uncomfortably at my conscience. I had allowed a dissolution of standards into my life; I saw where unchecked pride, restlessness, and sloth had closed off any real opening to grow into a mature Catholic adult and a devoted husband and father. Even after Tommy's parting words on the significance of carrying one's cross, I still too often carried mine like a toddler moaning over a splinter. Charitable acts and a spirit of generosity were scattershot. Attempts at virtue were not vigorous pursuits but damning half-measures. Of course, the sacraments produced saving fruit, but all too often, the sanctifying grace just seemed to hibernate. Though Loyola Retreat House rested among more than two hundred peaceful acres of rolling woodland, a shadow of dispiritedness followed me everywhere I went.

My post-retreat pattern had become like a scratch on a vinyl record that the needle wouldn't move past. During the retreat weekend, Christ would enlighten me on what was required to grow in virtue and move closer to His Sacred Heart. After a few Masses, Benediction, a series of penetrating talks, contemplative prayer, Adoration, and finally Confession, my soul would be stretched into such a state that I'd want to take on the identity of post-Pentecost Peter or blue-painted William Wallace. I ached to bolt home in a victorious gallop of renewed spirit and sanctity. But always—*every single time*—the burning enthusiasm and resolutions stoked on retreat would last only until I experienced my first irritation at home. It was a shameful realization, always reminding me of disgraced middleweight champion boxer Roberto Durán throwing up his arms and quitting mid–title fight against Sugar Ray Leonard.

So it was on this bitter, starlit night on the dock that I carried with me this heaviness; the retreat house had developed into what seemed a spiritually profitless weekend incubator. The homemade chocolate chip cookies, the restfulness, the stunning riverside sunsets, the renewed friendships with men, and the spiritual insights were satisfying to soul, mind, and body but had seemingly proven entirely ineffectual. Whatever it was—sloth, immaturity, or some other spiritual obstacles that prevented an encounter with God—I saw that I had become an impediment to myself. The most tangible consequence of this reality was, of course, its lacerating impact on Krista and our three young children.

But what discouraged me the most was that I *knew* God had repeatedly rolled out a red carpet of invitations to draw me closer to Him. Infertility, an arthritic body, Tommy's murder, several thousands of dollars lost in an adoption scam, and other devastations were His rescuing fires of refinement. I understood that God often operated most effectively by entering through wounds; that summer night on his back deck, Tommy had broken it down as clearly as one is able. God had repeatedly shown me that He wanted my soul close to Him; that He didn't want my eyes to wander from His. But I had habitually rejected the invitations. Once I had managed to navigate and triumph over a particular cross, I lazily let any intimacy God had kindled go to seed. Our "strengthened" friendship quickly became subverted and hollower than a dead tree. In the words of Johnny Cash, "there's no fence to sit on between heaven and hell."[1]

So on this dock, on this night, it became clear. If I didn't truly begin to fight for my soul and develop into the man God willed me to become, hell was a real possibility—no matter how infrequently my pastor, priests, friends, or anyone, for that matter, discussed it. Oddly, my thoughts didn't seem overwrought. Instead, they felt reasoned, perilously interconnected with logic, Scripture, and Catholic doctrine. I felt a preternatural indignation, as if God had become a night watchman looking down into my soul, reclined on a three-legged stool, stroking His beard and, with furrowed brow, slowly shaking His head. Perhaps Booth had felt this same way on this riverbank.

The tree needed to be kicked over. It came to me that God had sent His own Son to endure violence for each of His beloved created souls. So why wouldn't I want to fight for my own soul with the same violence? I knew that an acceptance of pain, in any manner God chose to administer it, would push me into grace.

He made the appeal to my soul, and the voice of the Spirit was clear: "Die to yourself, Kevin. Live in me now. Just come." I needed to be affected, annihilated for His grace, as was the heart of Saul when he traveled to Damascus.

Small waves slapped the dock, and the moonlight seemed like God's swinging lantern hanging down from heaven.

So, I requested a spiritual bolt of lightning: "Violence, God."

---

[1] "12 Quotes by Johnny Cash to Live By," excerpted from his autobiography, *Man in Black: His Own Story in His Own Words* (Grand Rapids: Zondervan, 1975), 14, posted at Oddessey, https://www.theodysseyonline.com/12-quotes-by-johnny-cash-to-live-by.

Tears fell, and, strangely, an overwhelming peace began to cover me.

After a long while, I stepped off the dock and began the climb up the hill to my bedroom. From out of the creek in the forest's darkness came a startling noise. A beaver cracked the midnight silence by slapping his fat tail on the surface of the water, which released a surge of chills that traveled the length of my body.

Exactly one month later, almost to the exact second, it seemed as if someone had flung a tomahawk into the back of my skull. My brain had hemorrhaged.

For the better part of a week, I was as close to death as I imagine one is able to be. One night, when I was throwing up inside an MRI tube, I couldn't tell nurses I was choking on my vomit because the sloshing blood in my brain had rendered me unable to speak. I was powerless. I had perfect clarity of thought, though, and this unpleasant consideration reared its head: *So, this is what it feels like to die. This is Your plan for my end.* After five days in neuro-ICU, I could hardly move. I often forgot how to breathe. During hallucinatory moments, I tore shunts out of my head and swiped at them as if they were clouds of late-summertime mosquitoes.

The hospital chaplain, Fr. Bill, told Krista a demonic presence had taken up residence in my room. Krista had already known it to be the case. Fr. Bill visited as often as three times a day to pray over and anoint me. He handed Krista a consecrated Host in a golden pyx and asked that she hold it above me so the demons would flee. He told her to pray continually for my soul and to beg St. Michael's help.

"So, this is Your plan for my end," I thought in my smelly, threadbare hospital gown inside the MRI tube that suddenly seemed like a coffin.

The Priests We Need to Save the Church

When a series of catheter embolizations failed to control the flow of blood, my chief neurosurgeon went down the dark alley he had hoped to avoid. He opened the back of my head to untangle the arteriovenous malformation (AVM) and remove the nest of vessels releasing blood into tight crevices in my brain. But the surgery failed. The surgeon couldn't reach the malformation. He told Krista that if he had proceeded further into my cerebellum, I would have died.

It seemed to most, then, that this would be my last day. Krista begged for prayers.

A priest by the name of Fr. Jim Stack, from a parish an hour away, answered the summons to anoint me. It was the right call. Not only was he Tommy's best friend, but he had just started a healing ministry, inspired by a mystifying, life-changing event he had experienced a short time earlier on his climb to the Shrine of Our Lady of Guadalupe in Mexico.

When he entered my darkened room, Fr. Stack and his healing assistant, Mary Pat Donoghue, had just finished praying the Chaplet of Divine Mercy and calling on the saints of Maryland. Since the surgery, I had been incapacitated and was unresponsive.

Fr. Stack—an old weightlifter and blue-collar priest whom Tommy had called Stackman—told me later that he bent down and whispered one question into my ear: "What saint do you want to intercede for you?" My response, he said, stunned him.

"Bring my uncle down," I whispered, my first words of the day. "I need Tommy now."

So Stackman stood up and started to call on his best friend.

"Hey, Tommy. Hey, buddy," he pleaded. "Kevin needs you now. He's calling for you to save his life."

What unfolded next was one of those miracles that slips through the back door because all the front doors are sealed shut.

What seemed a benevolent fire descended into the room, and Stackman and Mary Pat suddenly found themselves in the middle of something marvelous and supernatural. Both almost fainted. "There were lights everywhere," Fr. Stack said. "Everything in your room took on light. And all of a sudden, the presence of Tommy and the saints surrounded your bed, and everything took on a great warmth. I felt the whole heavenly court around you. It was overwhelming."

Stackman and Tommy collaborated well. The next day, I received an angiogram. It came back clean. The trapped blood and fluids had vanished; the AVM had disappeared. Doctors scratched their heads.

God's violence had run its course. I would be well.

Now it was up to me.

To appease the boredom of my long hours of recovery resting in bed, I decided to write about my experience of God's graces in brokenness; it was later published in a book.

Then I started to think more about Tommy—and more about the supernatural work of holy priests.

2

Hot Summer, Cool Priest

As ideas began to gather in my mind about the ordained men who bring the Blood of Christ into the souls of men, an old memory came back to life.

I was a few years out of college with a newspaper writing job I shouldn't have taken, in a lonesome backwater Florida town. I considered quitting and returning to Maryland a failure until a timely piece of advice rescued my flatlined career. "Kevin," a reporter told me, "when you enter a poor town with a reporter's pad, don't just write 'there were broken windows.' Count how many there are. Then find the people behind them." Thereafter, I mostly threw out my journalistic "who, what, and why" and started trying to dive into souls in order to pull out stories. It was then that my writing career finally took off.

Now, all these years later, after Tommy's transformative words on the purposefulness of crosses, his murder, and his otherworldly work in my ICU room, I found myself wanting to step through windows and speak to priests suffering from the fallout of scandal in the Church.

The desire to write for priests had been nailed to my heart in the days, months, and years following my failed brain surgery, after which I found myself with what seemed an entirely different set of eyes. Old interests—sports and D.C. political intrigue, to name just a couple—abruptly became hollow and lost resonance. It was as if my eyes now possessed a capacity to see through to the heart of things, sifting out insubstantial and transitory interests that had once held some value for me before a surgeon opened the back of my skull. A spiritual director might have suggested that a type of *sensus fidelium* had taken root within me, but I had neither a director nor any idea what the term meant. I did know I had survived a brain hemorrhage; many others have not. And I knew that, although surgeons and teams of nurses had worked wildly to fix my drowning brain, it was the work of two priests, two best friends—one dead, one living—that was most responsible for saving my life. I *knew* firsthand the authoritative healing power of the priest; I had experienced it. So I believed that what Jesus commanded of His disciples was possible: to heal every disease (Matt. 10:1; see Luke 9:1). Tommy and Stackman, as anointed men of God, were just doing their job.

I found it heartbreaking and appalling that people were flooding out of the Catholic Church in greater numbers than out of any other Christian denomination over the past ten years.[2] All too often in personal encounters, I found myself listening to bored pew sitters who told me they were considering giving up going to church or switching to the new, enormous nondenominational church down the road. Once, in a post-Mass Sunday-morning donut line, a mother with welling tears in her eyes told me she had given up the fight to get her teenage daughters to attend Mass. "They're completely tuned out, and when I finally can

---

[2] Pew Research Center, *Faith in Flux: Leaving Catholicism* (Washington D.C.: Pew Research Center, 2011), https://www.pewforum.org/2009/04/27/faith-in-flux/.

get them here, they don't see the light that kids need to see in a priest's eyes," she said. "They've stopped coming. And their dad's allowing all this to happen." A married couple we know stopped by our house while on a neighborhood walk to tell me they had left the parish because of a renewed energy they had found at a nearby Protestant church. I asked, "But don't you miss the Eucharist?" Their bemused look revealed that the Blessed Sacrament lived in the backwoods of their thoughts.

All the while, I kept thinking about priests and all the tools that they had at their disposal to help bring these people back to Christ and His Church. Practically speaking, I just wanted to point priests to their shepherding mandate, about which I had gained such intimate knowledge through Tommy. As priests of God, they possess supernaturality to pour out upon the souls of men and to build them up into saints. As one lone sheep in the pen, I simply wanted to implore priests: "You're God's poets. Help us to see His gaze of love through your lives."

I knew that, like us laypeople, each priest is a unique person. All sober-minded Catholics understand this reality. Anything I wrote to the modern-day priest couldn't be a clenched-jaw critical analysis; that would entirely counteract what I wanted to be a sincere appeal for priestly heroism in what often seems a dark age of Catholicism. My hope was simply to arouse in priests a nobler form of duty and selflessness in serving Holy Mother Church and in addressing her under-catechized, unenthusiastic, fleeing flock. It would be an invocation for hesitant but willing priests to consider a new form of martyrdom — the daily, gradual dying to self in order to save their dying flocks.

But who were the priests I would plead to in my writing? I begged the attention of the well intentioned, but struggling and timid priests in this post-Christian kingdom of modernism. But equally important as the *who* is the *why*. *Why* are these priests this way? Was it a lack of supernatural faith? Did they not think of themselves as central influences on their parishioners' souls? Were they just weak-kneed and crudely formed in seminary? Did they fear the judgment of the world more than God's? Or perhaps they had re-engineered the role of the Catholic priest according to their imagination to fit today's reigning worldview.

My goodness, how I knew our thirsting age panted for faithful priests in the mold of St. Peter. It sounds hackneyed, but I knew that priests like this had become the last of the Mohicans, in a certain sense. They were the sole social force insisting upon moral absolutes; they alone stood within modernism's wide valley of moral contradictions, societal revolution, and egalitarianism and pointed, everlastingly, to truth. Virtually every Christian faith had diluted two thousand years of revealed truths from Scripture and Tradition and tailored it to society's progressive pull. Each day, a swelling sector of the culture revised what treading the hard path of virtue looked like. The whole Western world, it seemed, howled in unison, "Come evolve with us! Or be cast out."

But God doesn't evolve. And I knew that priests ought to proclaim this truth as a sort of merry, house-to-house Christmas wassail, re-echoing the mystery of the Incarnation and the call to conversion to all those who crossed their paths.

It was zero-dark thirty outside their parish doors. It was time each of them acted accordingly. The center hadn't held. But a true shepherd holds his flock. It marks his identity.

So with this idea in mind, I began to write.

Then the summer of 2018 arrived.

It was perhaps ironic — or providential, depending on how you view things — that the greatest crisis of the Church hierarchy in Catholic American history began to rear its ugly head when my manuscript was more than halfway completed. I had interviewed dozens of bishops, priests, exorcists, seminary rectors, seminarians, and lay Catholics in the months before the breaking of the Theodore McCarrick accusations, the priestly impropriety and cover-ups detailed in the Pennsylvania grand jury report, Archbishop Carlo Maria Viganò's eleven-page bombshell letter alleging an immense homosexual Catholic clergy culture, and the ensuing landslide of breaking stories that detailed other sexual exploitations of adults and minors, including the abominable seminary abuses exposed in Chile, Honduras, and Argentina. Viganò requested that Pope Francis resign. When the pope was asked about Viganò's suggestion, he famously chose silence.

In the wake of revelations about the impiety, cover-ups, and disorderliness, a group of disillusioned Catholics began voicing their concerns in what seemed like the cacophonous soundtrack of the summer. A sizable number of discussions in my interviews with clergy skirted around and occasionally brushed up against the outer band of a category-5 hurricane—the dark underworld of clergy homosexuality—that had by midsummer thundered onto the scorched North American Catholic landscape. The hurricane's eye settled over the hot, humid Washington, D.C., metropolitan area, which was already being fed an insufferable amount of daily pre-confirmation posturing by politicians opposed to Supreme Court nominee Brett Kavanaugh. Details of McCarrick's bedding seminarians at a diocesan summer house and other behavioral deviancies seemed to arrive in overflowing buckets each morning, and tens of thousands in the nation's capital were dumbfounded; we hadn't known what so many bishops and clergy apparently had about McCarrick's serial predation. We saw and heard only his grandfatherly visage and measured voice. He had become the seemingly charming backdrop of our lives around the turn of the century as we raised our families and went to work each day—and in the aftermath of the Boston-led clergy malfeasance in 2002, it seemed as if McCarrick could be the safeguard to help guide the wounded Church in America as she limped forward. So, as he continued his seemingly unchecked trajectory in ecclesiastical responsibility, diplomatic weight, access to Vatican money, and public persona, Washingtonians remained blinded to the secret life that would lead to his laicization in February 2019. Stunningly, it emerged throughout the latter half of 2018 that Rome had been aware of McCarrick's sinful lifestyle for many years, confirmed by a series of firsthand accounts. The Vatican was under no illusions. This man had risen to the highest echelons in the world—a Catholic power broker whose backroom impurity and influence stretched like a black aura—with Rome fully alert to it all.

The veil of secrecy had been lifted, and Washington Catholics, and faithful Catholics worldwide, now understood what guardian angels standing watch had known for so long—something dark had infected the Church and was rotting her from within.

During those long, sweltering three months, reaction to the news of McCarrick's sins quickly began to spin into fury at his successor, Cardinal Donald Wuerl, who was repeatedly accused in the Pennsylvania grand jury report of ignoring or finding ways to circumvent priestly evil during his eighteen years as bishop of Pittsburgh. When Wuerl then suggested that *bishops* should be impaneled to investigate the scandals of *other bishops*, a brushfire ignited in his backyard.[3] This suggestion alone is perhaps what

[3] Peter Jesserer Smith, "Bishop: Lay Faithful, Not Bishops, Must Investigate McCarrick and Coverup," *National Catholic Register*,

sparked the lasting flames of the laity's revolt. A growing number of vocal and silently prayerful protesters descended on Wuerl's residence as the summer pushed forward. So he flew to Rome in the dark of a summer night to consult with his close friend, Pope Francis. "Talk with your priests," the pope told Wuerl.[4] But that would be no easy task; many priests had already lost all confidence in Wuerl's leadership; they indicated as much to me in interviews. By October, Wuerl was no longer the spiritual leader of Washington.

Although the time seemed ripe for a sackcloth-and-ashes penitential movement led by Church leaders, a spirit of charity and reflective humility seemed unnaturally absent. A reckoning of the disorder and offer of complete transparency never emerged. Perhaps bishops didn't realize it at the time, but by the end of the summer, they had seemingly killed off any remnant of their moral authority and spiritual fatherhood. Their piecemeal assimilation to American culture over the decades had done them in with intentional, Mass-attending Catholics. Pockets of disturbed Catholic laity were planning trips to Baltimore for the annual gathering of the United States Conference of Catholic Bishops in November. They wanted to greet the hierarchy in a manner they were not accustomed to.

August 6, 2018, http://www.ncregister.com/blog/pjsmith/bishop-lay-faithful-not-bishops-must-investigate-mccarrick-and-coverup.

[4] Michelle Boorstein, "Pope Francis Hosts Embattled Cardinal Donald Wuerl in Rome, Tells Him: Talk with Your Priests" *Washington Post*, September 5, 2018, https://www.washingtonpost.com/news/acts-of-faith/wp/2018/09/04/pope-francis-hosts-embattled-cardinal-donald-wuerl-in-rome-tells-him-talk-with-your-priests/?utm_term=.5503de817aa0.

The Priests We Need to Save the Church

A "Silence Stops Now" rally was organized on the waterfront near the hotel where the bishops gathered. Speakers there urged Church leaders to investigate those bishops who enabled Mc-Carrick to continue his homosexual predation of seminarians and priests. It was reported that some bishops paid for extra security.[5] Never in the history of America had the Catholic hierarchy faced anything like this.

In the midst of this upheaval, I sought to publish this simple lay-written book that proposed a blueprint for clergy heroism and stressed the pressing need for apostolic men attuned to souls. Even though the idea was to succor a beleaguered hierarchy and its priests, I prepared myself for criticism from publishers along the lines of *What gives him the right to tell a priest how to be a priest?* When indeed that happened, it was upsetting for me and for the many priests I had interviewed, who were heartened by the idea of an earnest Catholic man penning an aspirational book for priests.

One of these priests was a wonder-worker, Msgr. John Esseff, a ninety-two-year-old mystic regarded by thousands of Catholics as one of the holiest men in the world. He alone would become the reason I would continue to write and complete my seemingly orphaned book.

Twice, on the same winter day in 2018, I was asked to contact this priest. A prolific Catholic author, Patti Armstrong, and a celebrated local priest urged that I arrange a meeting with Msgr. Esseff, with whom I was unfamiliar. Both Patti and the local priest were enthusiastic about my book and were eager to help connect me with wise priests throughout the country. Both agreed,

---

[5] "Blood on the Walls," transcript from Church Militant, November 9, 2018.

though, that Msgr. Esseff was *the priest* with whom to speak. Patti gave me his phone number. "Kevin," she said in her charming midwestern accent, "you have to find a way to speak with Msgr. Esseff. I imagine that you've never spoken with a priest like him. I know he would want to hear what you're doing with your book. And I think he'd have some valuable things to offer you."

I phoned Msgr. Esseff and left him a message. When he didn't return my call after a week, I thought it was likely I'd never speak with him. But later that month, he did call; he had been on the road giving a retreat for priests. As I began to explain the premise of my book, he cut me off.

"I understand what you're doing, Kevin, and I'd like you to come and visit me," he said in a warm voice carved out of almost a century of prayer. "I'd like to see you in person to speak about what you're doing."

Then, surprisingly, he inquired, "Would you mind if I prayed for you and this book you're writing?" I had known this priest for all of two minutes. Snow was falling on lonely acres of southern Maryland farmland as he began to pray aloud in a voice as soft as wood smoke. At the time, I was driving down unplowed country roads to interview a certain priest who had assisted in one of the most grueling exorcisms in American history. His prayer seemed mystical—like an old piece of poetry dropped from heaven or from the lips of a gray-cowled Cistercian monk. After his prayer, we hung up.

Then he called right back.

"Would you mind if I celebrated a private Mass for you?"

"Uh ... Of course. Would it be a problem if my wife, Krista, came along?" I asked.

"Of course not," he said. "It would be my pleasure to meet her."

After disconnecting, I continued my drive to meet with the priest who had been scared stiff by a series of terrifying encounters with Satan.

I wasn't aware that Msgr. Esseff himself had spent half his lifetime exorcising demons.

In preparing for my interview with him, I discovered that there was likely no priest in the world who had spent more time with as many bishops, priests, and seminarians this past half century than had this venerable exorcist. For decades, he had been invited by bishops, seminary rectors, and pastors to travel the country and speak with clergy about the path to holiness. For many reasons, clerics are eager to meet him — but two stand out in particular. First, in 1959, he shared a two-hour conversation about prayer in a small Italian cottage with a *bilocated* Padre Pio. The holy saint, famous for bearing the stigmata, offered Msgr. Esseff his own guardian angel whenever he might feel the need for proper discernment while hearing confessions.[6]

Second, twenty years later, Mother Teresa became one of Msgr. Esseff's closest friends. After some years of traveling by her side as her confessor throughout impoverished areas of Lebanon, the saint told him to re-engineer his entire vocation. She asked that he begin to help shape priests.

"Father, I know you think it's your vocation to be with the poor and broken — but it isn't," Mother Teresa told him. "It is to form priests."

Since then, he has obliged the saint.

---

[6] "St. Padre Pio and Bilocation — Msgr. Esseff Describes His First Encounter," Discerning Hearts, podcast, 6:33, https://www.discerninghearts.com/catholic-podcasts/st-padre-pio-and-bilocation-msgr-esseff-describes-his-first-encounter/.

Msgr. Esseff lives on a hilly, tree-lined street in a quiet section of Scranton, Pennsylvania, where folks from the farthest reaches of America descend on his meager living quarters to encounter his holy manner and mystic voice. He is a spring in the desert for them. The day Krista and I visited, he had just finished meeting with a woman and her teenage daughter who told him their story of being under persistent demonic attack. Yet he approached us with a tender smile and embrace. His stooped-back shuffle, his shiny head, his bushy gray goatee, and his magnanimity lent him a warm, striking Yoda-like presence. He led us down the well-worn carpet into his parlor, which seemed a shrine. There, portraits of martyrs, and of his old friends Padre Pio and Mother Teresa, Marian artwork, images of the Fatima children, the Sacred Heart of Jesus, Saint Michael the Archangel, and the Divine Mercy image greeted us. Catching Krista admiring his portrait of three Fatima shepherds, Msgr. Esseff told her, "The demons hate Jacinta. They scream like hell when you mention her name. Jacinta's got enormous power. If only people knew."

Msgr. Esseff seemed like a defiance to these times. He was enveloped in a peaceful glow as he spoke of his upbringing in the Eastern Catholic Maronite rite, his devotion to the Blessed Mother and the Sacred Heart, and the pre–Vatican II days of his early priesthood, when he begged his bishop to allow him to take on an apostolate of serving the poor. "I couldn't wait to tell all the broken that they were loved by Jesus too," he said with a toothy smile. "That was the only mission I had for a long while. In fact, I still have it."

After relating some of the remarkable stories from his life, he turned his attention to my book—and the atmosphere of the room changed. The warmth and courtesy of his gentle voice departed as his thoughts traveled back into what seemed a malevolent shadow of memories. He began to speak of a heartbreaking landscape of malfeasance, omissions, and a seeming dethronement of Catholic teaching to which he had been exposed in American seminaries shortly after he had left holy Mother Teresa's side. It was a time, he said, when darkness was palpable within these institutions.

He walked us through a timeline of unholy land mines, describing the lack of discipline, the immaturity, and a homosexual strain he had witnessed in seminaries. He told us he had stopped visiting the majority of them long ago. What he began to see as a trickle of symptoms of disarray, he said, emerged as an awareness of abominations. Seemingly everywhere he cast a glance, he discerned that a spiritual crisis of malformed consciences and aberrant behavior had entered the Church to snuff out sacred traditions and erode souls. He voiced his concerns and warnings to seminary rectors, but more often than not, he was politely rebuffed. He soon realized that a closeted subculture *had been set free* to roam and deform the spotless Bride from within. A large crowd of post–Vatican II rectors and formators and many impious shepherds were not concerned guardians of the Church of God, Msgr. Esseff said; they seemed to have an unholy resolve to change it irrevocably. The long dark night of modernism that Pope Pius X had forecast at the turn of the twentieth century had arrived. And it wasn't set on moving.

"I began to see that the seminary was the sick womb of Holy Mother Church. Priests became deformed in the belly of the Church—or if you were a well-intentioned and good seminarian, you were going to be aborted. The guys who were real—they would just leave.

"I saw it as demonic. It was easy to piece together—when you're anti-Eucharist, anti-Mary, and anti-prayer, you're of the demonic."

Then he spoke about today's modern priest and his unwillingness to partake in the demanding but triumphant work of devoted prayer and unseen sacrifice for his flock.

"I'm a priest sixty-five years—and I'm very strong about this. We don't have a priest shortage right now, nor do we have a shortage of vocations," he said. "What we have is a shortage of priests who pray. We have a severe crisis in our priesthood because priests are not praying. They are not fathers. If we are to do anything well as priests, it must come from prayer, but we've stopped praying. Consequently, most of our priests seem to be bachelors today."

He exhorted me, "Kevin, you write this book. You tell them that, as a lamb, you need them to be a shepherd willing to die for you. Tell them you need a priest with a father's heart, not a bachelor who doesn't pray.

"If a priest doesn't truly love the Eucharist, there's no chance for holiness. If he doesn't love Mary, there's no chance for holiness. If he doesn't love prayer, there's no chance for holiness."

After he passed in and out of his theories on what led to the depth of depravity in seminaries and the priesthood—"this Modernism began to take root well before Vatican II"—he proposed the steps that he thought would bring the Church back to the fullness of unconstrained grace: unremitting priestly prayer, a luminous devotion to Christ's Sacred Heart and Mary's Immaculate Heart, and consistent priestly penances to succor their parishioners. "A priest must be a father who shepherds souls to heaven," he said. "A priest must be Jesus, who dies."

Msgr. Esseff then reminded us that he wanted to celebrate the Sacrifice of the Mass for us.

This Mass seemed of a different order, as if it were being celebrated by an apostle. It was bathed in a deep supernaturality, similar, I imagined, to those old family-room Masses celebrated in the shadowed light of a turf fire in the wilds of western Ireland. So enchanting was the experience that Krista's eyes began to well with tears at the start of the Eucharistic liturgy. When Msgr. Esseff slowly raised the host with fingers, hands, and arms worn down by arthritis and toil, tears ran down her cheek.

Noticing that Krista had been touched by the intimacy of the Mass, Msgr. Esseff began to speak softly with her off to the side afterward. She asked if he would anoint her. Inflamed with the love of a great-grandfather, he smiled and requested that they move into the sacristy. Ten minutes later, Krista reappeared with reddened eyes, dazed. He had given her a parting gift; he'd just read her soul. He had pulled memories from her as simply as he would have blessed our meal, revealing secret pain she had left in her wake long ago. He then offered specific direction on how to navigate through the uncured wounds of her past.

"Kevin, as he anointed me and looked into me, it was Jesus who was speaking," Krista said. "It didn't *feel* like Jesus. It *was* Jesus who stood in front of me. And he kept asking in a whisper, *Why are you running?*"

When we returned to Maryland, Krista told her spiritual director she had visited with Msgr. Esseff. A broad smile took shape on the priest's face, and he asked like a curious little boy, "Did you get your soul read?"

Forever moved by our visit, Krista spent time dwelling on all that Msgr. Esseff had exposed in her soul.

And I kept thinking about his words about those old seminarians—who were many of today's priests.

3

Be Vianney, Be the Curé

In the shadow of the Catholic Church's summer of shame, a prayerful and renowned Washington D.C.–area priest gifted me with a first-class relic of the world's lone canonized parish priest, the Curé d'Ars, St. John Vianney. It was a small drop of the French saint's blood. The priest had given me the relic when he learned of my desire to write about priestly heroism and the call for vocational renewal. He didn't realize the providence behind his gesture.

Months earlier, as I settled into the idea of writing for priests, I understood that it was necessary to explore their giants: the priest saints. My narrow thoughts, bullish ideas, and zeal merely endangered me with a prideful vulnerability. Conversely, I knew that priest saints carried uncommon weight; the Church recognized them as paragons. Practically speaking, I knew I needed to research, study, and prayerfully examine their sanctity, to see what had set them apart from their contemporaries and enabled them to become saints.

In addition to wanting to grasp the means and methods of priestly excellence, I wanted to learn how so much territory — especially relating to the practice of virtue and understanding sacred truths — had apparently been ceded by Catholic spiritual leaders over the past half century. I wanted to know why, for the past fifty years, as it seemed to me, the towel had been thrown in on encouraging lives of holiness in their flock. I thought that studying the lives of priest saints could reveal the noble manner in which priests used to fight daily for Christ and for souls.

One January night some time later, I realized from my freezing home office that my pursuit of comprehending priestly sanctity had turned into a pilgrimage. These lionhearted priests had escorted me into a graced countryside of heroism, where, one by one, they lined up in formation, a cadre of willing martyrs inflamed with love. I began to see these priests as sacred holy champions, with breviaries tucked beneath their arms, wearing wide-brimmed black hats, scuffed shoes, and weather-beaten trousers, as they stooped to ruffle an orphan's hair. Whether in fog-shrouded outposts, in isolated countrysides, in warring towns, on dark islands, or on cobblestone Roman streets (with the catacombs beneath), a superhuman eternal echo sounded from within these men: "Christ, lead me closer." Their simple plea was daring because these shepherds, with a supernatural sense, seemed to know that God's response would be to take them to places they didn't want to go — to villages that humiliated and rejected them, to starvation chambers, and to forgotten asylums of maggot-infested lepers who didn't know there was a God. They followed God to communities that slaughtered them, or, like Blessed Charles de Foucauld, to deserts, where it seemed as if no one listened to a thing they said.

And, of course, one notices in the lives of these holy priests their imitation of Christ in the Garden. *Your will, Father. Not mine.* Just as our Savior knew that He must die to save, so, too, were these priest saints willing to carry their crosses and give up their lives for the Faith. Many imitated Christ to the point of physical martyrdom, in order to uphold the Bride of Christ. Others chose a different, perhaps even nobler, route, integrating martyrdom into their lives by consenting to daily self-denial in order to guard and sanctify the souls of their parishioners. They mortified themselves bodily and immersed themselves in prayer to draw down God's sanctifying graces. They took on severe penances, disciplines, and toil to safeguard their parishes, islands, and villages against evil. They did not cede ground, and when they were tempted, they prayed themselves through it. They seemed to me sacred princes from lost places.

One day in August, the day after the release of the Pennsylvania grand jury report that tore into consciences like Old Testament plagues, I awakened at 4:00 a.m. and thought of Vianney. I sat at my writing desk, with the antique golden reliquary with Vianney's blood beside me like a monument of captured light, and I wrote a long letter to priests. Later that day, a website, *Catholic Lane*, published it, and within twenty-four hours, innumerable American priests and many from other parts of the world read my open letter, titled "Be Vianney. Be the Curé."

In my letter, I acknowledged the woundedness that shepherds felt when facing the disillusionment, anger, and rebellion of their flocks because of the sexual abuse convulsing the Church. I urged priests to turn their eyes to Vianney and the heroic manner in which he transformed the backwater of Ars into a sea of devout souls. By configuring himself to Christ through remarkable self-denial, round-the-clock availability, and humble love, he was able to revive Ars' Catholic identity, which had been garroted by the French Revolution. Under this emaciated, poorly educated country priest, the woebegone town found itself undergoing spiritual reconstruction. Townsfolk eventually fell in love with the uncommon priest because he absorbed the people of the lonely

The Priests We Need to Save the Church

French village into his heart. Thereafter, tens of thousands of French seekers streamed into Ars to lay their eyes on this holy priest, who spent more than a dozen hours each day absolving sin in his cramped wooden confessional.

In my column, I suggested immediate, practical actions that priests should take to restart the journey toward sanctification and the healing of their flock, based on the fascinating life of Vianney. My proposals would cause Satan to rear his head in a riotous fashion—completely at variance with his demons' subtle method of infiltrating the priesthood with homosexuality, clericalism, and indifference to souls. Since Vianney was forced repeatedly to face down the Enemy (especially in his bedroom at night), priests following in his footsteps should expect no less. Nevertheless, I implored them to "be Vianney; be the Curé." It would be the day-to-day holy witness of the parish priest—not the words or witness of the pope, bishops, theologians, or the most prolific Catholic authors, evangelizers, and educators—that would begin to heal the bleeding Church. But I wrote that until all priests made the decision to bleed themselves for the Church, renewal simply would not occur.

Just a few days after the publication of my open letter, a gregarious Maryland priest, Fr. Larry Swink, stepped out to preach on "that which cannot be named"—active homosexuality within the ranks of the priesthood. He told his parishioners the story of how he detected it on the first day he entered seminary, then of the manner in which it had been haunting the Church from within. Mass-goers said his candor about the plague of homosexuality and modernism in the priesthood was both startling and necessary. After his diagnosis of the problem, he cheerfully provided a clear path forward for his parish and for the Church to become renewed, centering his comments on personal holiness, self-denial, and greater time spent in front of the Blessed Sacrament. His Sacred Heart (LaPlata, Maryland) parishioners broke into sustained applause before he was able to begin the Nicene Creed. They knew they had a fighter committed to their souls and to the integrity of the Catholic Faith, which he was charged by God to sustain.

In the meantime, at another parish a few long country roads away, a different sort of priest announced in his homily that approximately 50 percent of all priests are gay — and that their sexual urges were natural and one of God's gifts. He said that the problems in the priesthood were due not to homosexuality but to the celibacy that priests are required to observe. He mentioned the dire need for female priests, asserting that women's nature better suited them to be Catholic priests. That congregation, too, applauded. Sides were forming, like the rising action in a Tolkien novel.

Later that Sunday, Fr. Swink went on a seventy-mile bike ride that ended at dusk. Still breathing hard after his ride, he told a friend, "When you start war with Satan, you'd better be in shape." He was only half kidding. Then he stepped into his rectory to wash up for a Holy Hour, a daily appointment he hadn't missed since his early days in the seminary.

A few days later, on an uncharacteristically cool August evening, twenty or so men and I gathered with our associate pastor and another recently ordained priest on a friend's back porch to air our grievances and express our incredulity over how men ordained to be our spiritual fathers had forsaken their identity with Christ, failing both God and us. The men were eager to know how many other atrocities remained hidden from the public. Our host, John, dropped a heavy ten-inch-thick binder containing a copy of the Pennsylvania grand jury report beside a cooler of cold beer and bottled water.

The Priests We Need to Save the Church

About an hour into the gathering beneath the stars, I found myself strangely bored with the animated discussion. Justifiably, men from the parish—many of them close friends—came to vent, propose solutions, and question how the Luciferian tide had so easily been able to crash onto their Church. One gentleman, Joe, finally bellowed, "Okay, so we know about the problems and the evil. So much of it is out there, but nobody is speaking to the solutions. What do we do with this? I don't think anybody really knows how to respond."

My boredom dissipated.

"I'd like to propose an answer, Joe," I said. "Priests need to be holy and to lead us to holiness. I think the answer lies there. What's happening with this scandal on a large scale is the same thing that happens in my heart on a smaller scale when I don't choose holiness."

I continued, "That's the real scandal of the Catholic Church today. Too many priests aren't calling their parishioners to true holiness. We've come here tonight to address the obvious public scandal, but Mary has been weeping over this sickness in our Church for a long time now. It seems to me that what sets us apart as Catholics has been contracepted by priests who don't preach the fullness of the gospel and the need for holiness—so, of course, we end up with McCarrick, the report, and all the rest of it."

After hearing Monsignor Esseff's startling diagnosis of many American seminaries and of the dangerous priests they formed, I had spent much time piecing together the manner in which the Church had been wounded and hollowed out from within.

I left thoughts such as these mostly unspoken that evening:

How could a priest reverence Mary, speak of her maternity, or even point his parishioners to her unique role in salvation history when he knew his own earthly mother would be ashamed of his secret sins, his tacit acceptance of them, or his half-hearted priesthood?

How would a priest be able to reverence the Body of Christ sincerely if he had quietly accepted illicit relationships among the clergy or the laity? If he didn't defer to God's commandments regarding the human body, how could he reverence the Spirit's movement in the Mystical Body at the Consecration? In the eyes of many Catholics, the Mass had been diminished by priests who seemed to give as much importance to glad-handing and small-talking parishioners on their way into Mass (a good thing in itself) as to the supernatural act of consecrating bread and wine, which become the Body and Blood of Jesus.

If, out of shame or laziness, a priest rarely frequented the sacrament of Reconciliation himself, why would he make appeals for his parishioners to go to Confession? If he was caught up in secret sin, which he chose to persist in, how could he address the seriousness of parishioners' sins? Did he even believe that God's graces for healing and change were efficacious at the moment of absolution? If he was an active homosexual, or accepted that lifestyle, or was simply too cowardly to address it publicly, how could he begin to explain without hypocrisy the benefits of a well-made confession?

And, as Msgr. Esseff had said with sadness, if a priest doesn't persevere in prayer, he certainly isn't going to mention the need for it in his homilies. Sermons on the importance of the family Rosary, the fruits of a weekly family Holy Hour, or even the need for a devoted prayer life are all but forgotten in Catholic America, because, as Msgr. Esseff said, many priests don't spend private, intentional time listening to God and speaking to Him themselves.

The Priests We Need to Save the Church

With these thoughts in mind, it wasn't hard to see how distinctive manifestations of the Catholic Faith would disappear over time: the venerable forms of the liturgy, the incense and the bells, the august quality of sacred music, and the faithful's awed reverence in the sanctuary, the Sacred Feast, and belief in and devotion to the presence of Christ in the tabernacle.

It wasn't hard to recognize how the diluted modern liturgy and a type of doctrinal revolution was able to spread its tentacles throughout the Catholic landscape. Rather than committing to live out sacrificial vocations configured to Christ for the glory of God and the salvation of souls, many priests, it seemed, had chosen to live for themselves, walling themselves off from the people they were meant to serve.

Throughout this arid summer, I experienced a regular impulse to spend time with Jesus in the Blessed Sacrament. He offered order, calmness, and light amid the confusion and darkness.

On one evening following our men's group, I found myself unable to shake an unusually anxious feeling in the Adoration chapel. Feedback from my open letter to priests continued to stream in. I knew that my enthusiasm for the Church's return to the purifying work of self-sacrifice, devoted prayer, and greater penances was heartfelt, but was it *correct*? Was my zeal for truth and my proposal for a way forward preventing me from identifying errors and mischaracterizations in my view? And as a member of the laity, what gave me the right to tell a priest how he should effectively shepherd his flock and live out his vocation? Dozens of priests and laity said they were emboldened by my challenge of dying to self and joyfully accepting the cross. A few said that they cried. Others, however, found my letter to be presumptuous and scolding. As a sportswriter, I understand that one of the primary roles of a columnist is to provoke countering viewpoints, so I wasn't struggling with the counterarguments as much as with my own heart. As the homilies of Fr. Swink and the other priest demonstrated, sides were forming in what seemed an unspoken schism. Some considered Archbishop Vigano's letter valorous, a document that would stand the test of time and eventually be compared with the most impactful words of the Church's greatest reformers. Vigano claimed that Pope Francis had full knowledge of McCarrick's homosexual lifestyle but ignored it. Vigano also claimed that the Holy Father freed McCarrick from the ministerial restriction that Pope Benedict XVI had imposed on him. But some bishops, priests, and laity dismissed Vigano as a curmudgeon and doctrinal rigorist with a vendetta because he'd never been made a cardinal. Francis's silence allowed Vigano's accusations to dangle menacingly on a clothesline that stretched across continents.

Some Catholic folks suggested that restoring litanies to the saints, parish Rosary processions, the Forty Hours devotion, and other Catholic traditions would be the springboard to begin to heal the Church and spur reform. Others scoffed, dismissing this sentiment as an quixotic yearning for a return to a pre–Vatican II mentality. I have to imagine that ambitious Catholics worldwide, consciously or unconsciously, began the process of examining on which side they fell. Everyone, it seemed, had a sense that *this thing* wasn't going anywhere for a while.

"The Church is undergoing a crucifixion now," a prayerful priest told me at the time. "We're going to suffer for a while, but even this is part of the suffering that Christ told us we'd endure."

I carried these thoughts to the chapel that evening, but rather than attaining clarity in the silence, my thoughts seemed disarrayed, as if emptied from a drawer in my head and dumped onto the floor of my brain. Attempts at prayerful meditation detoured off into what seemed like cacophony. I looked at Christ in the monstrance, hopeful that He might settle my thoughts and speak to my heart, but He remained perfectly noiseless. It was evolving into one of those nights when my time spent attempting to cling to Christ and to hear His voice seemed a waste of His and my time.

Finally, I decided to open the Bible beside me, flip to a page at random, and drop my finger down—a simple game of Bible roulette. I half-convinced myself that the verse I put my finger on was the one God wanted to whisper into my distracted ear. I hoped I wouldn't land on a weeping-and-gnashing-teeth passage.

I opened the brown softback leather Bible, flipped, stopped, and put down my right index finger, which landed on the final verse of this passage:

> A *Just Shepherd*—Woe to the shepherds who destroy and scatter the flock of my pasture says the Lord. Therefore, thus says the Lord, the God of Israel, against the shepherds who shepherd my people: You have scattered my sheep and driven them away. You have not cared for them, but I will take care to punish your evil deeds. I myself will gather the remnant of my flock from all the lands to which I have banished them and bring them back to their folds; there they shall be fruitful and multiply. *I will raise up shepherds for them who will shepherd them so that they need no longer fear or be terrified; none shall be missing, says the Lord* (Jer. 23:1–4, emphasis mine).

This passage described precisely what was in my heart. It was a direct hit. So, before Christ in the monstrance, I began to consider the shepherd about whom God spoke to Jeremiah. What did today's true shepherd look like? How would he act? What would he say to today's disturbed laity? How would he regain the trust of a Catholic world that had seemingly collapsed all around him? Would that Catholic world even follow *this shepherd*?

Sometime thereafter, a skinny Irishman named Declan Dinneny came to mind. He was the only actual shepherd I had ever known. I hadn't seen him in twenty years, but this farmer isn't the type one forgets. For starters, he could throw down a pint of Guinness faster than anyone I knew. He spoke in a wildly undulating, high-pitched voice and was as hard a worker as anyone I had encountered. When he spoke, I caught every fifth word. I fell immediately in love with him and his humble ways.

On two occasions, while visiting his kindhearted farming family in the hilly countryside village of Killeshandra in County Cavan, I watched as Declan whistled tunes and milked cows, slaughtered chickens, addressed his crops, baled hay, and drained pints at the smoke-filled corner pub at the close of day. My most vivid memory, though, and the one that most caused me to marvel, was the way Declan commanded his large flock of sheep. I consider myself blessed to have witnessed it. Interspersed between our conversation as we proceeded down a hillside path was his staccato burst of short, quick calls and whistles. For the length of five football fields of wavy green pastureland, he had managed to lead more than fifty sheep down a steep hill, across a country road, and into a pen carved into the pocket of a valley. No sheep dog was required, just Declan's voice.

He spoke. The flock followed.

Right then, on that August evening, as I knelt in front of the Blessed Sacrament, I recalled the man who had stood alongside me, also quietly marveling at the dazzling skill of Declan's sheepherding: Tommy. Suddenly, my uncategorized thoughts started to piece things together and bring clarity to the night.

The Priests We Need to Save the Church

Tommy had stood on that sun-splashed hillside next to me. He was the monument to the shepherd described in Jeremiah. He had revealed himself to thousands of souls to be that very shepherd. He had poured himself out tirelessly for his flock as shepherd of their souls. Those souls knew intimately the vitality and might of his priesthood. When I began to write for priests, I had dismissed the idea of memorializing my uncle, knowing he would have mocked me mercilessly for even considering it. Also, he had been gone for eighteen years. Although an editor for a Catholic publisher encouraged me to write a book solely on Tommy, I was reluctant, believing it an exercise in nepotism. It never took off.

Still, his presence, voice, and memory remained dominant in the Maryland–D.C. metropolitan area. After I wrote *Burst: A Story of God's Grace When Life Falls Apart*, hundreds of strangers lined up after talks and readings, not so much to share their thoughts on my book but to share memories of Tommy and the encounters with him that changed their lives. It seemed as if everywhere I went, people wanted to speak about the impact he had made. My large extended family had experienced the same thing. Countless folks considered him the most joy-filled and impactful man they had ever met. The year following his murder, the name Tommy spiked for newborns in the area. Knights of Columbus councils, Hibernian Divisions, school chapels, and parish halls took on his name. A Monsignor Thomas Wells Society that would financially support future priests formed the year after his death. A thoroughbred racehorse owner named his chestnut gelding *Tommy Wells*, and he won his first race.

I convinced myself that night that it wouldn't be an awful idea to bring Tommy's memory back to life. If nothing else, it would be a fun exercise to consider how he'd have taken on the summertime upheaval and how he'd have steered the Church toward authentic renewal.

Why not?

I walked out of the small chapel feeling buoyed. The sun was setting behind the bluff filled with lowing cows, and Tommy felt a millimeter away. *Uh, Keggy, a really dumb idea—but let's see what we come up with anyway.* Ill-mannered, but seemingly a millimeter away, suspended in a late-summer breeze and copper sky.

The next day, my old reporting instincts went into gear. I began to track down dozens of Tommy's parishioners, high school and college friends, fellow seminarians, and priest friends to arrange meetings. Whether over the phone or in person, I had two common experiences.

One was that, when many of these folks spoke of the impact Tommy had made, one after another they became overwhelmed and broke down. I was surprised that some of the men I met with had to excuse themselves temporarily or apologize as they worked through tears when attempting to explain the lasting footprint Tommy had made in their lives. During phone conversations with people who knew Tommy, voices suddenly broke and trailed off into silence. I spent quite a bit of time waiting for men and women to compose themselves.

The other common factor in these conversations was that people remarked, "You know, Fr. Wells is who we need today" or an equivalent statement.

But why Tommy? What made him unique? Was he that special?

4

Tommy: The Happy Martyr

An arctic blast had descended one January night, but the antique
boilers in the basement of Our Lady of Lourdes Church basement stayed true; they hummed mannerly in the background.
Sleepy newborns were snug in this gathering place. More than
a dozen happy children, awkward teens, Washington profession-
als, mid-forties married folks, and others up to eighty years or so
had stepped onto the outdated checker-tiled floor and into the
enfolding warmth to remember the man some folks call America's
happiest martyr—Tommy. All these years after his death, they
always return for this annual gathering of the Monsignor Thomas
Wells Society.

The old-style La Panetteria restaurant has brought in heaping aluminum pans of portobello ravioli, lasagna, chicken parm,
and steaming bowls of angel hair pasta. A line of eight giggling
children ready their serving spoons. Dark winter ales and a se-
lection of modest red and white wines have been brought in by
folks to help make the night merrier. After all, this is a night of
quiet cheer, consideration of traditions, and commemoration
of a dearly beloved priest—so homemade cakes, cookies, and
pies have made their way in, too. They're all here—we're all
here—for Tommy, and for the newest batch of seminarians whom

the society is helping with its prayerful and financial support. Some here tonight are pursuing a cause for Tommy's canonization, but he would have laughed out loud at the idea and called it a scandal to the Church.

Most here don't know the ins-and-outs of Tommy's early life before he was a Catholic priest. One of his nephews regales the gathering with family lore handed down over the years. The listeners lean in with undisguised curiosity, closely following the information that might lead to a deeper understanding of how he became who they knew him to be.

Over and over at the dining room table in his 1950s Washington, D.C., home, young Tommy and his siblings listened as his Catholic-convert father, Stanley, an engineer and building contractor with a fascination for philosophy and the saints, rained down questions on morality and virtue. Occasionally, Tommy answered correctly. Thereafter, he developed a taste for great Catholic writers and thinkers. On long strolls home from school, the pool, or a friend's house, his slightly pronounced nose was buried in the pages of good books, which fostered friendships with Hilaire Belloc, G. K. Chesterton, Walker Percy, and many of the saints.

Eventually Tommy gravitated to the light of St. Augustine's *Confessions* and *City of God* (books he dog-eared, marked up, and underlined). Augustine had him journeying to the mountaintop of Plato and Aristotle, where he drank in the interconnectedness and orderly manner of reason and the principles of natural law. Wellsprings of wonder and logic began to pool in his mind. His thirst grew, and he set out on a journey with the early Church Fathers, who gradually made him realize that he needed to carve out a new identity for himself: he needed to become another Christ, as a priest.

His parents, the priests and parish family at Blessed Sacrament Church in Chevy Chase, the great writers, saints, theologians, philosophers, and an ear attentive to the voice of God had all transformed him. "It was part of the air that I breathed as a boy," Tommy said in a video, speaking to seminarians. "It was pure gift. The whole environment spoke of the goodness of God." They had led him to focus increasingly on a single mystery: Christ disguised in a small, circular piece of bread.

The Body and Blood of Christ had drawn Tommy in the manner of a heavy-headed sunflower that bends in the direction of the sun's rays and becomes splendorous. He had fallen in love with Jesus in the Eucharist, and he wanted to be near Him now, always.

On the long drive back to Boston College during his senior year, Tommy made himself a hard promise to harness every bit of his courage and break the news to his girlfriend seated beside him. *By the time I get to the bridge up ahead, I'll do it.* They crossed the bridge. "I want to become a priest," he told her. He told me that the remainder of the car ride was quiet, except for periodic tears from his ex-girlfriend.

Shortly after graduating from college, Tommy entered Christ the King Seminary in Upstate New York, where his devotion to God, His Church, and the Eucharist deepened.

From his ordination by Cardinal Patrick O'Boyle on a cold, rainy day, February 13, 1971, Tommy's mission was written large on his heart and made unmistakably clear: he would attempt to lead parishioners to heaven by raising high the Body of Christ, the blazing torchlight that would be their guide. He found his sustenance and fullest identity as a priest when transforming bread and wine into the Body and Blood of Christ. It both fueled and exhilarated his interior life for each of the twenty-nine years of his ministry. The strength of his priestly interior life and the sacrificial love he poured into his flock were in direct proportion to the intensity of his devotion to the Eucharist.

Each time he elevated the Host after the Consecration, his visage and manner famously transformed and seemed to reveal the awe he felt at being permitted to lift Jesus heavenward. Those few moments offered parishioners a glimpse at a raw and sweet intimacy; it seemed as if their pastor had withdrawn from the altar, the church, the town, and even the world and had been transported to Golgotha, beneath the cross and the pearl-black afternoon sky, and then lifted up into the wound in Jesus' side, near His heart. As his gaze stayed transfixed on the elevated Host, Tommy whispered secret poetry. Deacons, lectors, and altar servers could eavesdrop, but the language was foreign. If you attended one of his Masses, you simply could not miss it—hundreds of people have mentioned to me over the years the impact that *this moment* had on them. They could clearly see that he *knew* he held Jesus in his fingertips.

The explosively joyful manner of Tommy's homilies inspired thousands of hearts over the years, but the manner in which he reverenced the Eucharist moved souls. It wasn't cheap opera; it was an organic sharing of his soul. This mystical unfolding at Consecration, in fact, triggered the desire in a few awestruck young men to pull up stakes and leave steady girlfriends, budding careers, and relaxed lifestyles to turn over their lives to God in the priesthood. Even today, when these priests elevate the Host, it seems as if Tommy has climbed into their bodies. At least one of them whispers thanksgiving to Tommy each time he holds the Host aloft.

At a time when many post–Vatican II priests seemed to be de-emphasizing the Eucharist's supernatural presence, Tommy made the decision to celebrate the Sacrifice of the Mass each day of his priesthood precisely because of it. If he was allowed to step into the heart of the mystery of transubstantiation, he would do it each day of his life. And if someone thought it Catholic hocus-pocus, a ceremonial memorial, or if he doubted the mystery of transubstantiation that takes place on the altar, Tommy would engage him forcefully to enlighten him. "What makes you think you got it right, and Jesus had it all wrong at the Last Supper?" I recall him thundering. One gentleman told me that his life was changed when Tommy vigorously challenged him: "What part of Jesus' saying, 'This *is* my Body and Blood' don't you understand?" The man went on to become a priest.

"The Body and Blood of Christ was his entire priesthood," remembers Fr. Greg Shaffer, a parish employee whom Tommy had led to the priesthood. "And because of that, he saw everything with a heavenly vision. If he trusted what happened with the Eucharist at the altar, then he was going to trust God with everything else.

"Obviously, with all those hundreds of friends he had made and all the people who loved him, you could tell he was in this world—but not really. He saw everything with transcendence. Everything here and everything that took place was somehow attached to God."

In the Washington, D.C., area, my uncle was perhaps as beloved a priest as there has ever been. It is easy to see why: the people Tommy served saw him as a joyful father intimately attuned to their souls, always offering his prayer, his warmth, and his availability. His parishioners knew he would do *anything* for them. They saw that he simply desired that they grow in grace and learn God's will for their lives. He told them not what they wanted to hear but what he believed Christ wanted them to hear.

As their spiritual father, he strove to guard their souls from evil and would even suffer for them if necessary.

My uncle also decided early in his priesthood to radiate the joy of Jesus Christ. His effervescence and the cheery folksiness of his manner acted as a bulwark against gloom. "The priesthood is fun for me," he said in the vocations video, "because it gives me the opportunity to sell the most wonderful thing that God has to offer—that is to say, to sell His Son, Jesus Christ. Now, that may sound corny, but it isn't.... Invariably, I would say almost on a daily basis, I have the kind of opportunity to really invite people to change their lives—and to me, that's fun."

You could walk into Tommy's presence brokenhearted or ready to pick a fight, and then walk away wringing cheer out of your clothes. He knew what St. Teresa of Calcutta knew: "Joy is a net of love by which you can catch souls." To maintain this exuberance, he spent many hours in mental prayer. When he fell into prayer at one of the chapels at his many parishes over the years, its atmosphere could suddenly feel like midnight in Gethsemane, at variance with his sociable nature. His intense prayer life, motivated and fed by God's grace, allowed him to spend time generously with parishioners and to reap a rich harvest of corporeal and spiritual works each day. He understood that his priestly output had to draw from a wellspring. The work of a priest, he knew, was rendered valueless if it was deprived of its source of power.

Tommy also knew that in order to guard the souls in his care, he would be required to leave the safe shores of contentment and make himself *available* to people. Because of that awareness, he seemed to want to pour himself out for souls. He reasoned that if Jesus had offered Himself up to a bloody death to atone for our sins, then he, too, needed to offer himself as a victim. To Tommy, the most authentic path to this victimhood was to be unreservedly available. He offered himself up everywhere in appealing to the restless heart. And in this self-emptying, he seemed to discover the depths of his calling and his identity; Tommy would live out the slow martyrdom of availability. Sixteen-hour workdays were common. When asked, he often blamed his bleary eyes on hay fever. I imagine he often asked God to help him love the cross of long days.

The rhythm of those days was spent in entering into parishioners' suffering and loneliness, visiting hospitals, encouraging vocations, hearing confessions, teaching classes, leading retreats, and getting to know his flock at their homes. Because his bishop continually transferred him to ailing parishes, he made thousands of friends. He told me that he received invitations to someone's home for dinner virtually every night of the year; he wisely made the most of those evenings, using the rhythm and mood of the night to work at winning hearts for Christ. He knew it was at the dinner table that hearts could be melted and changed, so he tried to be a window through which one could climb to reach Christ. He came at people with Irish effervescence, humor, and a crashing way that was mercifully free of pretensions.

He could approach parishioners, strangers, and passersby from myriad angles, penetrating them with his blazing cerulean eyes, full of candor and wisdom. When he met an intense thinker and a reluctant believer, he'd square his shoulders and go toe to toe with him in plumbing the depths of reason and order. Those with a sense of humor he'd charm with this blazing wit and storytelling. He'd listen patiently to why a person might hate the Catholic Faith and then strive to find the element of the Faith that would speak to the person's heart. Throughout it all, he wanted to proclaim that joy in this life is achievable and that it begins with knowing that Jesus Christ desperately loves us. He'd point to the cross. "See how much," he'd say with his smile, shaking his head. Simply put, he wanted to offer souls the peace that the world cannot give.

"He was the most joyful man I ever knew," Fr. Stack said. "He was the best priest I ever knew. He just got it. The joy of the truth of Christ lived in him; you couldn't miss it—people wanted what he had."

Tommy knew that living an authentic Catholic life and meeting the demands of divine revelation could be a difficult and often lonely task for his parishioners, especially because he understood the distorting power of the evil one. He knew the subtle manner in which Satan works to lure souls. Tommy's younger sister, Mimi, shared countless brief phone conversations with him over the years "just to break up the day and laugh out loud together." One day, her big brother didn't laugh. It was a moment Mimi will never forget. She had unwittingly told him that her kids had been playing with a Ouija board, unaware of its significance. He exploded on her. "He cut me off immediately," Mimi said, "and he said, 'What in the world have you done? Get that thing out of your house now!' The way he reacted told me that he knew evil was very real and that he had seen it up close."

He hated the thought of a wandering soul. If he caught the whiff of mortal sin in a parishioner, he encouraged immediate confession. He understood that each soul was singular and unrepeatable, so he fought to help save it from darkness. He loathed the habitual rot of serious sin, and dreaded it, too, because of its calamitous effect on the soul. If a person felt in exile or lost in a period of sin or doubt, he reminded that person that the Holy Spirit lived within him. His care for souls was tender yet ferocious because he knew every person's heart hungered to know Jesus and to respond to His call to holiness. He tended to his parish like the pacing Bethlehem shepherd, binding up wounds with the sacraments, with his joyful example, with the Word of God, and with piercing homilies that slowly and powerfully settled into consciences and changed lives.

Tommy was attuned to the priest saints' call from past ages to be prepared to suffer, and even to lose his life, in order to protect the soul of even a single lost sheep. If he was going to hold parishioners to a higher standard of holiness, he knew that he had to lift himself higher. He did so by becoming a servant, finding harmony in placing the welfare of his flock above his own. I imagine that he rarely considered weekly collections, parish goings-on, his own measure of comfort or degree of toil before first thinking through the state of the souls at his parish. A part of him lived in a state of self-forgetfulness, in which he thought no longer of his own life but of Christ's life within him. If Vianney—again, the Church's lone canonized parish priest—could spend as many as sixteen hours a day in his tight confessional unburdening souls, then Tommy, too, could take heroic measures and deep dives for the flock in his care.

As he grew stronger as a priest, so did his loyalty to even the thorniest teachings of the Faith—he was unafraid to preach on contraception, abortion, modernism, mortal sin, evil, hell, the Last Things, and other topics that priests often sidestep. He knew the treasure of truth, and he knew that care for souls required that he proclaim the full gospel, in season and out. If he encountered angry folks overtly antagonistic toward Christ, he told them they were on a path to hell. It was partly because of encounters like this he took on the nickname "Boomer." If something was true and needed to be said, he was going to say it. And if a growing societal hegemony had made it increasingly difficult to proclaim eternal and indelicate truths, he was going to proclaim them even more strenuously. His was a countervailing voice, an instrument intent on passing on the same sacred words given by Jesus to the apostles and passed on to heroic descendants of believers.

Tommy thirsted for the conversion of each troubled person he encountered, constantly reminding each one of the bottomless sea of God's mercy and of the fruits that came from a devoted prayer life. It was a different time, of course, from ours. Tommy gave hard noogies to smart-mouthed and disrespectful teens, bringing soaring egos back to earth. He'd shake his head in that teasing way, grin — *tsk, tsk, tsk, tsk* — and encourage them. "C'mon kid, sharpen up," he'd say, and the teen would rub the sore spot, smile, then fall in line. Because he was humorous and could spin a tale and hold court, many young Catholics came to regard him as a "cool" priest; but he didn't want that, and he was unafraid to exhibit his "uncool" ways. He consistently refused to sacramentalize marriages for couples who were already living together and those who weren't attending Mass or taking the sacraments seriously. Catholic couples who were shacking up may have dismissed the consequences of their living arrangement, but he did not — for he knew the cumulative effects of grave sin. If a Catholic had made a decision to tiptoe around the demands of the Faith or to customize it to fit his lifestyle, Tommy would unleash rebukes on that individual — not to humiliate but to fight for his soul and build reason into it — *especially* when the individual showed no desire to do so for himself. Yet somehow, none of this was off-putting. In fact, Tommy's untethered manner may have helped him make more friends and guide more lost souls back to the Church than any priest ever had in the Maryland-D.C. Corridor.

The reason?

My uncle wanted to be their father.

"We are half-hearted creatures, fooling about with drink and sex and ambition when infinite joy is offered us," C. S. Lewis said, "like an ignorant child who wants to go on making mud pies in a slum because he cannot imagine what is meant by the offer of a holiday at the sea."[7] Tommy wanted each of us to set out for that blissful holiday at the sea.

But the sea is roiling today.

Each of us needs an anchor. After Robert Paul Lucas murdered Tommy nineteen years ago, it took me some time to realize that I had lost my anchor. I found it again by meeting with numerous priest friends and former parishioners who loved Tommy and who had been influenced and encouraged by his words and the witness of his vocation. In the process, I discovered that the priest I need is the priest everyone needs.

My uncle Monsignor Wells was the happy shepherd willing to die for his sheep, and he never forgot that he needed to be among his flock. He embraced the simple, time-tested disciplines of our Faith in complete and selfless service to the Church. When a priest does this, he throws open the doors to God's graces and brings hope to souls, regardless of their circumstances. Holier priests lead to a holier Church. The true shepherd reveals the love of God in how he loves his people.

A good priest knows that he is ordained to be another Christ, and, like Christ, he is willing to die for his spiritual children. A priest who sacrifices like a father changes everything. That sacrifice is the key that's able to unlock every door in our post-Christian culture to free those trapped by the spirit of this world.

---

[7] C. S. Lewis, "The Weight of Glory," in *The Weight of Glory: And Other Addresses* (New York: HarperCollins, 2001), 54.

5

Holiness and Victimhood: The Lone Paths Forward

If the priest is a saint, the people will be fervent; if the priest is fervent, the people will be pious; if the priest is pious, the people will at least be decent. But if the priest is only decent, the people will be godless.

—Attributed to Dom Jean-Baptiste Chautard

"Get out of bed early, and get to the problem job. Eliminate every excuse, and work to turn it around." These words have been honored as the first commandment of the family masonry contracting company for sixty years. Long ago, my wise grandfather was emphatic about this message as he shared it with his son Dan, my father. My father passed on his father's words to his sons, and I imagine that one day one of my brothers will impart them to his son.

Our alarm clocks awakened us Wells men before dawn over the years, and we well understood that nothing heartening would greet us as early-morning darkness broke into light to illuminate a troubled job site. Whether forced to tear down recently constructed work, redirect a discouraged foreman, plead our case to a recalcitrant superintendent, or address any other number of obstacles, we knew that a certain penance was demanded of us before job-site renewal could take place.

And always this thought arose: "What did I do to contribute to this mess?"

The Catholic Church finds herself filled with trouble today. In the midst of it, I've often asked myself: "Did I contribute to it?" My shamefaced answer is yes, when I chose to live as a half-hearted Catholic. At the core of my failure is an awareness that I have not sacrificed enough for Christ's Church, which is now mired in a sickness that seems to have eaten into her very bones. My prayer life, spirit of asceticism, and charitable works have been haphazard and lackadaisical. I've rushed through Rosaries, slacked off during Lent, rolled my eyes interiorly during homilies, and shamefully refused to empty myself and fight for the souls of my children—to name a few omissions that have contributed to the unsafe listing of the Barque of St. Peter. I am one reason the Church has been so disfigured with impurities. I have not suffered enough for the Church to bring her into the world and even into my family.

On a broader level, the shift from a Church built on Christ's sacrifice to one of lax sensuality and unruffled comfort seems to have softened most of us. Saints used to write with human skulls on their desks as a reminder of death and hell. Today, society has been overrun with the happy-face emojis that seem to tell us, "All is heaven." Although innovations have given us greater comfort and convenience, nothing about an authentically lived Catholic life should be easy. But since many clergy have largely stopped calling for daily self-denial and heroic virtue and have not taught clearly what Catholic identity, sanctity, and committed prayer mean, Catholic laypersons present their Faith to the world in little more than a symbolic and superficial way. Symbols demand nothing of us; they denote meaning according to personal preference. Both clergy and laity must resolve to configure themselves as sacrificial, substantive "signs of contradiction" both interiorly and in broad daylight.

But as I argue in these pages, the faithful priest who decides to make himself a sacrifice for his parish helps to sanctify and save each soul within it. Sacrifice is the demand of the priesthood; when it is lived out, everything changes.

The sacrificial priest must lead us; his soul will have no true pleasure in this life until he forfeits his comfort and decides to lay down his life.

"It is not possible to create esteem for the priesthood except through an admiration for the priest's victimhood," Archbishop Fulton Sheen wrote. "No mother brings a child into the world without labor. No priest begets a vocation or makes a convert or sanctifies a soul except under the shadow of the cross."[8]

When we make victims of ourselves, we most resemble Divinity hanging on a cross. And we least resemble Jesus when we make ourselves comfortable—and that, ultimately, may be the principal reason our Church agonizes today. The great majority of Catholics and too many bishops and priests seem to have steered away from the fundamentals of the Catholic Faith and instead have given themselves to superficiality, comfort, and weakened devotion—and therein lies the paradox; if clergy fail to suffer willingly with Christ, then Christ's Mystical Body, the Church, suffers. It suffers from the effects of sin, disorder, and fatherlessness, all of which Jesus became man to set right and redeem.

[8]   Archbishop Fulton Sheen, *The Priest Is Not His Own* (San Francisco: Ignatius Press, 2004), 59.

"Unless the hands of the priest are scarred hands, Christ's mercies do not so readily pass through them," Sheen wrote. "Blessings, power, healing and influence get clogged by worldliness."[9]

On the eve of His Passion, Jesus spoke to His first priests about the only way forward:

> I am the true vine.... Remain in me, as I remain in you. Just as a branch cannot bear fruit on its own unless it remains on the vine, so neither can you unless you remain in me.... Whoever remains in me and I in him will bear much fruit, because without me you can do nothing" (John 15:1, 4–5).

Nothing has changed.

Full disclosure: as a Catholic layman, offering a blueprint for how modern-day priests can "get it right" comes with no small measure of awkwardness. When I was a baseball writer, I would never have dared to tell Wade Boggs how to handle Mike Mussina's change-up. I wouldn't advise my equine-loving wife on the secrets to navigating a tighter turn on a Hunter-Jumper equestrian course. They needn't hear from me because I would have offered nothing they didn't already know. For years, when I conceived of writing this book, I continually stuffed it down, threw it into the cramped closet of my mind, and pushed on with other things, as a thought similar to this repeated in my mind: "Don't. You have no right. You're not a priest. You're a layperson who stinks of sin (see wife and kids for long lists of substantiation)."

So, again, frankness is in order here: How dare I?

I dare because I speak in solidarity with many millions of ashamed and angry Catholics, reeling from audacious sin that

---

9   Ibid.

has been allowed to flourish within the Church for so long. Too many churchmen have profaned, insulted, and trampled on a sacred heritage that generations of hardworking, everyday Catholics fashioned their lives around. With these members of the laity, I love and need noble priests. I need their counsel, their guidance, and their holy example, as do all the laity in a world rapidly becoming paganized around them. So I dare to tell them, as a lone sheep from the pen, why their flock is fleeing, and I beg them to reconsider their role of shepherding their sheep back to the pen.

This book is a wholehearted plea meant to encourage the earnest priest who cares deeply for his flock and wants nothing more than to help lead them to everlasting life with God—but in this time of mistrust and disillusionment can't find the proper footing to shepherd them properly. It's an appeal for him to recognize and reclaim the mystical unfolding of the Holy Spirit on that remarkable day when he lay down before his bishop—nose and kneecaps pressed hard to the cold floor—and climbed into the skin of Christ. It's a plea for him to give birth (or rebirth) to the supernaturality born in him that day, the same mystery that propels him to help save souls through a vocation brimmed with an intense interior friendship with Jesus.

With today's aggressive secular push for individual autonomy devoid of divine moral law, the world (wittingly or not) is starving for brave, eloquent proclamations of the eternal truth. And Catholics need vigorous priests to strengthen them in a society that considers some of their strongest religious convictions hateful and revolting. As obedient servants *in persona Christi*, priests know they've signed up to be gallant, invigorating proclaimers of what Jesus proclaimed for three years to all who were willing to listen.

The Priests We Need to Save the Church

This brings to mind something I experienced at a men's retreat while writing this book. A young priest told a story to ninety-two men; I imagine that all ninety-two will not forget it. "The other day, we were having a great time at my dad's birthday," the priest began. "I wished my old man happy birthday. So he comes up to me later and says he wants me to be around for another forty or so years, so I can go on to be a good old priest one day. I said, 'I'm not gonna make it to old age, Dad.' He said, 'What are you talking about? Your health's fine.' I said, 'I'll be martyred by then.'"

This priest spoke this like someone requesting cream for his coffee. I think I know the reason for his casualness: he has a devout faith, has handed his priesthood over to Mary, has committed himself to a daily Holy Hour, and has worked mortifications into each day of his life. He is funny, handsome, athletic, and masculine in the truest sense of the word.

He is a man. And he knows that men who strive to redirect a secularized population will suffer. He knows that much of the world already despises him for his firm Catholic teaching. As time moves on, this priest believes that anger directed at him and his style of priesthood will only intensify. He told me that he is consistently mindful of Jesus' words: "If the world hates you, realize that it hated me first" (John 15:18).

A haze surrounds us today like an invisible poisonous gas. Any sincere Catholic off the street could mount an argument that a number of Catholic priests have simply chosen to forget or purposely abandoned the idea of offering themselves as a sacrifice. Our shepherds have at their disposal the cure for every single form of spiritual cancer, but for years too many seem to have chosen not to implement it, with an unspeakably harmful consequence: disordered or malformed Catholic consciences roam like millions of antelopes grazing in fields amid crouched lions. Sermons that skim truth's surface and conform to the culture show that luminous Thomistic thought and even pedestrian Catholic teaching on virtue, faith, reason, and morality seem to have been jettisoned. Is the toothless homily, which for half a century has avoided the tougher aspects of Catholic teaching, the very reason we find ourselves frozen in this winter of base morality and this cultural shift toward godlessness? Pew Research polls in the past few years have repeatedly shown plummeting numbers of Catholics, who seem to pour out of the Church like the Israelites out of Egypt. The excessively laity-friendly manner that steers clear of sin while straightjacketing the call for virtue seems to have resulted in emptying pews and gutted Catholic churches—where neither the afflicted soul nor the individual who sincerely desires to grow in holiness is moved an inch closer to sanctity. Perhaps even more tragic, due to her corruption, very few want to join the besieged Roman Catholic Church today. Too many see her as having succumbed to evil.

When I covered baseball, I'd often examine the multitiered farm teams to determine what prospects might eventually be able to add value to the Major League team. The promise of our Church's "farm system"—our Catholic youth—is unclear at best. As a father raising kids, for too many years I've played bystander and watched the Church's children seemingly become orphaned by socially conscious, doctrine-bare catechists—leaving them to choke on firehose-fed secularism. The unforeseen consequence of this impoverished catechesis is a devastating landscape of youth in desperate need of the Heimlich, which indifferent shepherds do not provide.

Our society is fast achieving the diabolical "flip"—virtue is now sin; sin is virtue—and hordes of Catholic children and teens are wandering. Our youth have lowered their heads not in sorrow and pain but to genuflect to Instagram, Snapchat, and Facebook, in order to turn away from their unspoken confusion, torment, and hidden sin. But truth doesn't live in social media, so their immortal souls further petrify in Satan's relentless spiritual war for them. And because it seems as if many Catholic dads and moms have decided to canonize comfort—helicoptering every aspect of their children's lives except their souls—their children are left unequipped to combat spiritual enemies. It seems as if many parents today would never conceive of fasting or spending a sustained time in intentional prayer for their bad-mannered, sulking kid. Often they just scream back at him. Many parents have made gods of sports, leisure, and fitting in. Suddenly caught up in a traffic jam on yet another mad dash to fetch Johnny at lacrosse practice, they automatically reach for their cell phone instead of the rosary dangling from the rearview mirror. Throughout their days, they instinctively and repeatedly find ways of not being or *seeming* Catholic. I know I do.

The priest must enter into this real-life grind and spiritual amnesia that we laity are living. Too frequently, though, he doesn't. It's as if a heavy mist or lassitude has contracepted his conscience and dulled his sense of obligation to preach hard truths, propose methods of attaining holiness, and embrace the "burden" he vowed he would to his bishop at his Ordination. Is it just absentmindedness—or indifference to the souls before him? Many priests seem coldly dislocated from the reality that Holy Orders made them into giants—they are other Christs, touched interiorly by the finger of God and able to help safeguard human souls and anchor them to God. Too many, though, seem to have backpedaled from speaking the truth. I've often wondered how often these priests meditate on their own supernatural fate and on the fate of the souls of their flock. What might happen if they did?

I know priests who've made the sanctification of souls the signature of their vocation. In modeling Jesus at the well—rather than sanitizing the sin or wrongheadedness of the Samaritan woman (see John 4:4–42)—these priests have unmasked inherent wrongs, proposed holier ways of living, and left permanent imprints on lives. Souls seemingly bound for hell have been detoured. I know more than a handful of people who've told me they'd have ended up in hell if not for the work of a priest.

"It's absolutely no fun preaching on sin to save souls. No priest in his right mind likes doing it," one priest told me. "But it does seem to work every time."

The radiant life of *this* priest rotates around his adoration of Jesus Christ in the Blessed Sacrament, an adherence to sacrifice and holy behavior, and an unceasing impulse to lead each of his parishioners to heaven—but the centerpiece of his vocation is his identification with the crucified Christ. It's there where he finds his vocation's tenderest fruit. His willingness to suffer rejection, long hours of unseen prayer and service, and a life set apart produces an infusion of graces for his flock. He becomes a saintly model, and in response, his parishioners begin to imitate him and desire to lead lives of sacrifice. This sacrifice-based union of shepherd and flock becomes a stunningly intimate partnership of grace. It is within this endless loop of self-surrendering love in imitation of the crucified Christ that *the* medicine to help heal the Church is brought to light—priest sacrificing for his flock, the world, and the Church; flock sacrificing for their priest, the world, and the Church. It seems only within *this* dynamic that the one, holy, Catholic, and apostolic Church will re-emerge as the beacon she was intended to be.

The Priests We Need to Save the Church

In my research for this book, which included a study of priest saints and the lay folks who have spun in their orbit, I haven't seen this approach fail. A desire for the supernatural is hardwired in us by God, and when the laity recognize in their pastor that supernatural dimension of mission, identity, inflamed love, and ardor for souls, they'll knock down cement-filled cinder-block walls to grow in virtue. But if a priest lacks this supernatural identity, his parishioners nearly always will remain unchanged. When a joy-filled priest proclaims the Faith boldly and clearly as the very blazing furnace of truth it is, it is responded to in full. But when the message is stripped down to conform to modern sensibilities, no one is inspired, and the unsettled war within us between right and wrong pushes on.

This retrieval of priestly sanctity has everything to do with priests leading a return to sacrifice, Adoration, and the untiring pursuit of holiness within themselves and their flock. Every priest saint understood that his sanctity directly impacted the laity. Happy-face symbols do not grace the annals of Church history; martyrs, saints, and heroic priests and nuns do.

"For a long time, it was thought that only monks, hermits, and Desert Fathers should be holy—and that one didn't typically think of the parish priest as being called to such holiness," said Msgr. Stephen Rossetti, an exorcist, educator, and prolific author who has written several books on the priesthood. "But today, this can no longer be the case. The parish priest is called to become holy, to commit himself to a life of integrity. I regularly tell this to seminarians. A lifetime of self-giving, Eucharistic prayer, and holiness should be expected of the parish priest.

"As we move forward in time, we may be a smaller group of priests, but I think we will be holier, and we will be battle-hardened. The priest's devout prayer, integrity of life, and firmness of faith in the face of persecutions and rejections will lead the way. One holy priest can change the world; the Devil said as much to St. John Vianney."

At the Last Supper, Jesus spoke aloud to His Father about His first priests gathered around Him: "I revealed your name to those whom you gave me out of the world. They belonged to you, and you gave them to me, and they have *kept your word*" (John 17:6, emphasis added).

Ten of those priests died for Christ.

How many would die for Him today? Would I?

In meditation and prayer, I've come to see the following eight characteristics of priests who have *kept their word*; this priest with these eight characteristics is *the priest I need*, the priest the world needs now. His vocation isn't marked by cheap grace; there is only the call to sainthood and an impulse to help move souls toward heaven.

The identity of this priest has taken further shape after many interviews with clergy and laity, and through seeing close-up the fruits of conversion brought about by Tommy's priesthood. This priest is attuned to the souls of his flock who have become vulnerable to sin and endangered by the enticements of today's post-Christian culture. Because persistent courage and zeal for truth live immovably within him, this priest compromises nothing for the salvation of their souls. He has resolved to accept hardship for the sake of his flock, and in a very real way he dies bodily because of it, through extended hours of work, scheduled fasts, intensified prayer and works of mercy, and decreased sleep—but isn't that what a loving father does for his children? A father does whatever is possible to keep his child from leaving the path of abundant life.

So what is the essence of the saintly priest? I took this question with me, again and again, to meditation, to Adoration, to

Rosaries, and on quiet neighborhood walks over the past year. I am certainly not an infallible arbiter of priestly excellence, but the following individual characteristics repeatedly came to mind:

The saintly priest

1. Adores the Eucharistic Jesus
2. Is devoted to Mary
3. Prays devoutly
4. Assumes a victimhood
5. Is a father
6. Is persistently available
7. Preaches divine truth
8. Dives into souls at a moment's notice

The first four characteristics (explored in chapters 6 through 9) allow a priest to *receive* God's grace; the other four (explored in chapters 10 through 13) are things a priest must *do or be*. The first group lays the foundation of his priesthood and initiates the second group—traits that mark a priest's magnanimity. Although each of the traits bear upon one another ontologically, it would seem impossible for a priest to flourish if he refuses to receive God's grace through regular Adoration of our Lord, devotion to our Blessed Mother, a devout prayer life, and a spirit of asceticism. How could he act upon the will of the Father if he doesn't receive it—if he doesn't know what it is? If the priest, however, does welcome God by receiving the assistance of the Holy Spirit, his vocation will become not only effective, but sublime. It will allow him to help many souls reach heaven.

The remainder of this book will unpack personal thoughts and include stories on the saintly priest—the one Catholics thirst for today, the one who will begin to rebuild and spiritually sustain our Church: the priest I need.

Happily, there are innumerable cheerful, contemplative priests helping to keep the Church afloat by waking up each morning willing to die for her. These are the holy ones among us. They seem to have extra light in their eyes, a joyful confidence unhidden in their character that reaches deep into souls and shapes eternal destinies. Christ shines in them. They know that participation in the priesthood demands identification with the crucified Jesus; they know that it's this reality that presents the truest image of Christ to their flock and to the world. Their message to the laity is emphatic: Christ came to die, and we, too, should unhesitatingly desire a self-emptying or death to self, dying to sin and to the unabated allures of the world. Faithful priests know that it's only within this type of interior revolution, an amputation of self-will, that their vocations will bear good fruit. They contemplate this *dying way* in the quiet of candlelight most days of their priesthood. There is no other way for them. Yet they don't present themselves as emaciated desert hermits or killjoys; instead, they come off as the happiest people in the world.

This appeal for priestly sanctity has its root, of course, in my upbringing, subjectivity, and zeal, but it has also evolved by mining deep into the biographies of the heavenly court of the priest saints. The sacramental energy generated by these eight priestly traits, I believe, would also have been valued by two of our great modern-day female saints—Thérèse of Lisieux and Faustina. Their souls and interior prayer lives were formed by priests such as this.

The Church, the Mystical Body of Christ, has modernized. But the priest's duty to point to her invulnerable, sacred heirlooms has not changed. Only when the priest wholly surrenders his life to God as a type of sacred expiation will his flock be nourished with lasting food for the journey. Holy priests have understood their reparative role for millennia. Accordingly, as they've undergone torment in addressing debauched behavior, distorted philosophies, and mortal sin, they've managed to break down the walls of apathetic flocks, enter in, and convert them. "Holy priests sanctify their people; unholy priests, except for a miracle of grace, turn people away from God," said Fr. Gerald Fitzgerald, who led an apostolate for helping beleaguered priests. "God, after his own self, after his own incarnate self, has no more powerful means of saving souls than his priests. As a matter of fact, he counts upon his priests to give his sacramental self to the Mystical Body."[10]

The laity certainly claim no connoisseurship on the priestly path to holiness, but as baptized members of the Church, they participate in the royal priesthood of Christ (1 Pet. 2:9). Their voice is vital. Catholic experts, clergy and nonclergy alike, are calling for the lay faithful to play a major role in helping to spur our priests to holiness. Theologians offer studied treatises. But everyday Catholics speak from their souls, a wilderness voice unmatched in its authenticity. Theologians, philosophers, Catholic educators, and others simply cannot duplicate the fervent but mostly untapped voice of a thirsting laity.

Archbishop Fulton Sheen esteemed the enormous value of the laity's voice: "Who is going to save our Church? Not our bishops, not our priests and religious. It is up to the people. You have the minds, the eyes, the ears to save the Church. Your mission is to see that your priests act like priests, your bishops like bishops and your religious act like religious."[11]

---

[10] Fr. John Hardon, S.J., *A Prophet for the Priesthood: A Spiritual Biography of Father Gerald M. C. Fitzgerald* (Inter Mirifica, 1998), 69.

[11] Elizabeth Scalia, "How to Restore a Church in Scandal? Begin with a Collective Confession," Word on Fire, August 2, 2018, quoting Archbishop Sheen in his address to the Supreme

The second half of this book is a collaborative effort with Jesus, because at its heart, it is only for Him and His Mystical Body that I write. And, of course, there's the disquieting possibility of this scenario unfolding on my judgment day: "Oh, and Kevin, that book about my priests?" as he slowly shakes His thorn-scarred head. That thought has given me pause—as has what God once mentioned to Doctor of the Church Saint Catherine of Siena as she was praying one day: "Do you know, daughter, who you are and who I am? If you know these two things you have beatitude in your grasp: you are she who is not; I am He who is."

So there's that aspect, too.

So how *does* an old sportswriter and contracting supervisor manage a united writing effort with God, proposing to priests the way out of these low-clouded days of Church disarray, spiritual drowsiness, and laity disorientation? Gusto gets one only so far. God had been preparing me for years, I believe, by prodding me to empty myself of myself. He has detached me from the answers of the physical world by helping me to live the Church's teaching on in vitro fertilization; He has asked me to accept the murder of a holy priest and guide; and He has allowed me to survive a near-death experience because of the intervention of two holy priests. God knows I'm a slow learner, but He also knows I'm up for answering the call that has lived within me for years. So, trusting reader, please know that I've tried to continue to empty myself by following the standards set by holy priest saints when they begged for divine illumination—through increased self-denial, penance, prayer, and greater amounts of meditative

Convention of the Knights of Columbus in June 1972, https://www.wordonfire.org/resources/blog/how-to-restore-a-church-in-scandal-begin-with-a-collective-confession/21499/.

time spent before the Blessed Sacrament. Fed by His graces, I know there will be a better chance of hearing the Divine Spirit dwelling within me.

At its heart, this written plea is a grand ballroom failure if it lacks authenticity and is of little value to clergy, seminarians, and laity. If it rings as needlessly provocative or injudicious, then I have wasted your time and mine. With that awareness, I've taken a rather commonsense approach to go to Christ more frequently in the Mass, in the sacraments, and in Adoration, as a worker bee accelerates his services for his queen as the springtime draws near. There is great music in God's silence, and if I'm not cracked open so that God's voice can be poured into me, then I've failed here. Every thought contained in these chapters should be in accord only with His holy will.

This book simply asks priests to die in order to promote life. The request runs precisely in line with what they pledged to God at Ordination.

This book pleads for a priestly revival; it begs priests to help save the soul of the world.

"Mere duty is not sufficient for a true priest. He needs something higher: sanctity," Pope St. Pius X said. "Jesus Christ requires a simple Christian life of the faithful, but of the priest He asks a life of heroism. And, therefore, if Christian perfection is an ornament, a glory and a halo for any member of the faithful, for the priest it must be his normal way of life."[12]

More than a hundred years after Pius X spoke these words, with a Church in the midst of an identity crisis because of evil,

---

[12] Pope Pius X, *Recipe for Holiness: St. Pius X and the Priest* (1959), available at Catholic Tradition, http://www.catholictradition. org/Priests/priesthood2-1.htm.

hidden sin, and failed leadership, we look to heroes such as Pius X, who guarded the rich Deposit of the Faith by choosing courage, steadfast holy work, and prayer over comfort. And in a personal way, I look to Tommy now, who daily worked at gaining a foothold in consciences so that souls might be redirected and saved.

If you're a priest struggling to find courage, if you've developed lazy or sinful habits, if you've embraced a misshapen view of your priesthood, or if you feel you've yet to experience God's power in your priesthood, you know far better than I that God's mercy is wide — that Lazarus of Bethany once rose from the dead.

You are needed now.

Here's a story of one priest who came home.

When I met this priest and he began to tell his story, I imagined the worst eternal outcome for him. But as he pushed forward with the tale of his corrupted priesthood, I began to see that God had continually dropped into his life invitations for renewal — each one ignored. Then one day, everything changed. Satan had moved into his life.

Today, all that perverted his priesthood is gone. He's no longer the same man or the same priest. Nothing is the same now or will be again — the long thorns of pride and distortion have been pulled out. When more than nine hundred demons took possession of a pure soul he had been spiritually directing — some of whom called out his hidden sins, habits, and secrets in the voice of a leviathan — he came to see that hell was real and that he might one day reside there.

"I knew I needed to change radically," the priest said. "There's no going back to the old, happy, simpleminded priestly way. Today, I am a priest who strives for holiness and wants to save souls. I've glimpsed the supernatural world. In that world, there are hideous creatures."

The Priests We Need to Save the Church

This priest's vocation had been born in the wake of the tempestuous postconciliar era, the sexual revolution, and the release of Pope Paul VI's encyclical *Humanae vitae*, which reaffirmed the Catholic Church's teaching that using the body's natural rhythms of fertility as a means of family planning—and not contraceptive measures—was the morally appropriate manner to regulate birth. When Catholic University of America professor Fr. Charles Curran unleashed public rejections of long-held Catholic moral teaching at the university in 1968, crusading busloads of like-minded liberal theologians, priests, and nuns joined forces in Washington, D.C., to give voice to their dissent. Television stations and newspapers pursued the Catholic revolutionaries, and the Catholic Molotov cocktail of relaxed Catholic thought became the talk of much of the world. Then it spread.

Many progressive theologians and priests pointed to the fourth constitution of the Second Vatican Council, *Gaudium et Spes*, which ambiguously addressed the Church's "scrutinizing the signs of the times and ... interpreting them in the light of the Gospel." They relied on the document to bend two thousand years of Catholic thought into a new moral theology that eschewed natural law, which many believe was the cause for Church leaders and priests eventually to descend into depraved behavior and a seeming loss of faith in God. Priests secretly married, and others dated—men or women. An even greater number dragged New Age philosophies, reinterpretations, and corruptions into the liturgy, discarding traditions, sacred art and music, and the call to sanctity.

In the backwash of this era began this handsome priest's ministry in the 1980s. He had discerned his vocation after immersing himself in the Charismatic Movement within the Church. He said he felt a sustained "warming of the heart" in those days. He entered a liberal seminary, where he continued to rely on his "warmed heart" to illuminate and guide his ministry as a future priest. This warm, consoling afghan, he thought, would manage to cover whatever mission field Jesus would assign. No seminary professor told him that his time in the seminary was meant for human and spiritual formation, to ready himself for the uninterrupted demands of his chosen vocation. Hardly mentioned were the sufferings, the frequent long and lonely days, and multilayered burdens a priest is often required to carry. The Blessed Mother was virtually ignored. Prayer was whatever one wanted it to be, however one chose to define it. The priest learned at his seminary that the daily duty of praying the Divine Office didn't have to be so, well, daily. Or, for that matter, prayed at all.

So naturally, when he was ordained a priest, he mindlessly steered his priestly attention and efforts on what would engender that warmth. He hungered for the cover of what seemed to him the enfolding touch of God's manifest love and approval of his ministry. And he was very happy, or at least he thought he was.

When his polished oratorical skills, wit, mannerliness, and keen intelligence drew praise, warmth flooded his heart. He eventually was transferred to a high-profile parish in the heart of a tony section of Washington, D.C., its congregation sprinkled with liberal-minded, pro-choice Catholic politicians, left-of-center media, and the jet-setting crowd. As hearty pats on the back, firm handshakes, admiration, and exclusive party invitations increased in volume, pride began to spread its tentacles to all parts of his body, masquerading as sunny surges of Christ-kissed consolations. As long as he steered clear of thorny Catholic issues and stayed floppy or muted on inflexible moral teachings, this trendy priest seemed downright "saintly" to his celebrity parishioners. One of the world's most famous politicians at the time frequently lavished praise on him for the gracefulness of his homilies. Christmas "donations" were generous.

"All of *this* has a way of quietly tuning out the desire to become a prophetic and good priest," the priest said to me much later. "You're not thinking much about your own mortal soul — let alone of the souls you were anointed to look after."

One afternoon, he attended the Ordination of a seminary friend in Seattle (a man who has since left the priesthood). Recorded sounds of whale calls and chiming bells played throughout the Mass. But these were different times — so why shouldn't the underwater cry of a blue whale be included with the bestowal of Holy Orders, he thought? With a few days to himself following the Ordination, the priest decided to take a long drive in his rental car down the Pacific Coast to visit a female friend he had met during his time in seminary. Since that time, the woman had gotten married and was now raising her family in a small farming community.

Shortly after entering their small home, he felt an unusual depth of warmth, alien to the warm sensation he had come to know so well. This feeling struck his core. He found the small children to be happy and obedient, with a spirited radiance. His friend's husband was humble and hardworking. And his friend seemed bathed in a peace that flowed into every room she entered. He realized that nothing in their home seemed superficial. In fact, he had forgotten that such homes existed. Every action was genuine, of right order, and seemed to spring from the heart, like rays of warm sunshine stretching throughout the small house. He felt he had stepped into another dimension.

Then, a question came from his friend: "Father, would you like to lead us in the Rosary?" He told them he hadn't brought his rosary with him.

"What they didn't know," the priest admitted to me, "was that I didn't know how to pray the Rosary. I didn't even know the Mysteries. I basically thought the rosary was just women's jewelry. So I just told them I'd sit with them during their family Rosary." They all fell to their knees and began praying the Rosary. It was then that a foreign voice seemed to awaken within him, one that began calling him home to a purity and life of grace he did not know.

The next day, the whole family attended daily Mass together. "At first, I thought, 'Oh! Isn't this cute and quaint. They're going to Mass and praying the Rosary together as a family.' Then I spent a few more days with them, and my thinking changed. An overwhelming sense of joy came to me because of this family, who I thought was living the old way of Catholicism. But what they were showing me was a living, breathing example of a joyful Catholic family life. Here was joy. Here was truth."

Upon returning to his "hipster" parish, the priest felt compelled to incorporate his newborn Catholic awareness into his established, progressive priestly way. Almost immediately, though, he fell back into his old habits. Reorienting his priesthood and incorporating a devoted prayer life proved too cumbersome. He felt hopelessly inadequate in mustering the necessary courage to shed his prideful behavior. The Oregon family had, however, pricked his conscience and unchained a new interior voice. Now, shamefully, he regarded the warming of his heart as the sham that it was.

"I finally saw that what I experienced during the charismatic days and the warmth I experienced [in Oregon] as needing to be interlocked," he said. "I just didn't know how — or want to — bring the two together."

The priest eventually received a transfer to a country parish in a remote area of the state, where he was introduced to his predecessor, who would shortly be relocated. His parish seemed to belong to a different spiritual universe. He repeatedly saw the priest rise before dawn to make a daily Holy Hour. The priest wore an easy smile, had a bushy beard, and dressed in a long cassock that whipped when he played soccer and baseball with kids in the schoolyard. He seemed to always be in the chapel, praying the Rosary, poring over Scripture, or busy with a work of charity. He watched the priest celebrate Mass with a mystic's reverence. He saw a man who resembled Jesus.

"Once again, initially, I was put off by him because of his style of priesthood. He was *too much* of a priest," the priest said. "He had something that I simply did not have. But after he transferred, I saw that what he had drew me. He had a stability to him. His prayer life consistently came first in his life. Here was a priest who prepared his own soul before he tried to present the Faith to others. Prayer and devotion were always first for him. So once again, my mind was taken back to the [Oregon] family."

When he decided to begin to reform his priesthood, to imitate the life of the departing priest, he knew he needed to account for the vast landscape of his moral failings. He visited a holy Discalced Carmelite priest and confessed the nest of sin that ranged from childhood to the present day. Thereafter, he began to pray the Rosary and celebrate the Mass with greater reverence. He increased his prayer life and began to spiritually direct high school kids—but he still felt himself adrift. The Catholic devotions didn't feel connected to his soul.

One evening, a devout teenage girl who was considering religious life told him she was seeing monsters. Within a few days, it was determined by the large city's chief exorcist that a wild chorus of demons had taken possession of her soul. Satan didn't want to let this girl go; he wasn't budging. So, over the course of the next year and a half, this priest assisted the exorcist to help drive out the demons that had infested and seized control over this worn-out young woman. Throughout this time, Satan occasionally unmasked the priest's past shortcomings and mocked him. It was humiliating; he had nowhere to run or hide. That old *warming of the heart* in the face of this depraved, malevolent force was a disgraced and pitiful remembrance.

"There is an intensity of impact on the human soul when it is confronted by demons, when Satan stares you down. When you see demons and what they're capable of, there comes the reality that there is most certainly a hell. Becoming aware of this dimension changed everything in my priesthood.

"I'll never go back to where I was. I'm just going to be a priest from now on—a real priest."

6

The Eucharistic Glow

Patient reader, I intend no irreverence as I dare to juxtapose the motivation of the priest's daily Holy Hour with the stunning fidelity of a baseball player, who moved me as a child and later as a sportswriter.

I once wrote about a strange and striking man, Cal Ripken Jr., who, to many tens of thousands of boys, seemed a free-agent infielder on loan from heaven. He limped to his car alone under the stars after a game, then legged out a double the following night. Bruises vanished in a day. He often played when it looked as though a hot poker was knifing into his spinal column. When his knee felt wobbly after having his leg taken out on a double play, he knew a trainer would apply ice at midnight, so he ground his teeth and stayed in the game. Always in his subconscious sounded the call of tomorrow.

The shot-and-beer city of Baltimore swooned for Cal for one reason more than any other: his allegiance to his daily work. He refused to take a day off. The city's blue-collar symphony of bleary-eyed cops, bricklayers, short-order cooks, and the like understood that this Olympian-like figure had committed himself to them and to his duty—and they adored him for it. Hardy souls respect hardy men. They knew that, in Cal, they had a bridge to a working-man, black-and-white past. Day after day, this Iron Man became a Moses-like Exodus figure sticking it out until the honeyed end—surrendering his bodily aches, slump-enduring mental anguish, prolonged road trips, awful teams, and monotony of 162-game seasons to do all he could to help the Orioles win. In the midst of his grinding fidelity, he decided he'd never sit one out—so, for 2,632 consecutive days, he showed up to serve. For twenty-one years, the left side of the infield became his factory floor. Such a streak will never be replicated.

I sat in the press box on the evening he finally clocked out. On October 6, 2001, it seemed as if all of Baltimore cried. Cal's final trot from the dugout to his position at third base is an image I won't forget because I imagined in that trot the many thousands of times he had traveled that same path as a little leaguer, a high schooler, a minor leaguer, and an Oriole. Monuments in his image have since been carved for the most mundane reason in the world: he simply showed up for work each day. It was the effect of that fiat, though, that sparked the admiration of millions.

"I realize that the streak was never about the streak," Ripken said. "It was about giving all I could."[13]

I know a handful of priests like Cal. For several years, decades even, they've made a daily Holy Hour before the Blessed Sacrament; they are the most influential men in my life.

Here is one.

Before dawn broke this morning, a priest awakened as most of his seaside neighborhood still clung to sleep. As is his custom, he got out of bed, readied himself in the dark, and then

---

[13] Cal Ripken Jr., "The Streak," *Players' Tribune*, September 1, 2015, https://www.theplayerstribune.com/en-us/articles/cal-ripken-jr-streak-orioles.

proceeded from his small bedroom into the very Presence of Jesus Christ—incongruously hidden as a seeming full moon of sacred bread. This daily pilgrimage of Eucharistic devotion has changed everything for this priest. Each morning, he retraces these steps to rest his head on Jesus' breast, to spend an hour in candlelight before a monstrance, to reorient and renew his mind as he readies himself for another day of parish life. Often, he'll just sit and accompany Jesus, awaiting even a single word whispered to his soul.

"As a priest, so little works for me unless I spend this time with Him," he told me. "Everything begins and ends with this Mystery. He speaks to my soul here in Adoration. So it's where I want to be; it's where I have to be. It's where my priesthood gains its heart. And I'm not worth too much as a priest without it."

Behind the monstrance in his small chapel is a window that overlooks the sea and a fog-shrouded island in the distance. All is silent here except the lapping of small waves and an occasional call from a seabird. The sun begins to raise its head out of the sea, easing its early light into the priest's attic chapel. Jesus' Presence surrounds, penetrates, and commingles with the priest's body and soul. This tender tribute of veritable romance has become the consecrated secret of his priesthood and his entire life.

"The Eucharist was the only reason I became a priest. I knew it when I was eight years old. It's been more than thirty years since I've been ordained, and I've celebrated Mass every day since," he said. "And I've spent this time at Holy Hour in the same way. The whole heavenly court is somehow here with me. They're there with me when I raise up the Eucharist, and they are here with me, too, at Adoration."

This seaside priest has known remarkable suffering. After residing for several years in the lowlands of depression, he has learned to present himself at Holy Hour as a beggar, politely pleading that any mental weight or spiritual poverty might be lifted and carried away. His time with the Blessed Sacrament has rescued his priesthood. In humility, he has fashioned this daily retreat on one idea: simply to love with the faith of a child. So, he has learned to melt into his Holy Hour, during which he attempts to quiet his body and mind, even slowing his breathing and heart rate, to promote a stillness that, on good days, lets him leave behind the minefield of his thoughts, parish gossip, misplaced affections, worries about church debt, and even the troubled souls and hardened hearts he'll encounter later that day. He has learned that he's unable to handle the burdens of his parish and priesthood without this hour—so he begs for grace to pierce him.

At Adoration, he says, everything unhealthy and blasé in his priesthood is burned away by veiled light. And when he finds himself to be settled and bathed within this divine sea of light, he begs for resolve—even for interior revolution—so that he can fully adopt God's priorities, rather than his own. His twofold action is to forget himself and meditate on Christ's will for him. He's at home here in this grace of friendship, knowing that any litany, lyric, or spontaneously majestic prayer that rises within him has been placed there by the Holy Spirit. He is forever Ginger Rogers to the Lord's Fred Astaire, following the divine lead in a joyful dance. It's Christ who prays the prayer that already lies within him. This singular operation of grace is humbling for the seaside priest; instead of fishing for just the right word or pearl of wisdom to present to his King, he knows it is Jesus Christ who casts His line to reel him to Himself.

"He's taken this old dishrag and washed it clean at Holy Hour," he said. "He does the work. I just try to hang on."

His unbroken weeks and months of daily Adoration might be his most heroic act of loyalty and service for his parishioners because of the twofold purpose this sacred time serves: it increases his identity as another Christ, and it helps to guard the souls of his parishioners.

Priests have told me that time spent adoring the Real Presence—a practice many believe stretches back to third-century Egyptian desert hermits—is simply a response to the call of Christ's heart, a call that guides the whole of their priesthood. Their ministry, they say, bears little fruit apart from this committed time of enlightenment, warmth, friendship, and peace. They believe that each morning truly starts with their soundless procession to God, their tabernacled roommate. "Apart from me you can do nothing," Jesus told his disciples (John 15:5).

"I'm drawn to the Divine Master," said a priest who committed to a daily Holy Hour thirty years ago to overcome a spiritually dry seminary. "He's life-giving and refreshing. It's at Adoration that my priesthood takes its shape."

Even still, perhaps with an eye to multilayered pastoral and administrative obligations, it seems as if many priests have swept the Holy Hour into cobwebbed, monastic closets, considering it an unnecessary medieval Catholic relic and an inconvenient cramp of priestly style in these modern times. But in low-ceilinged basement rooms, Cistercian mountaintop cells, rectory boiler rooms, unused church offices, consecrated rectory bedrooms, in candlelit, stained-glass chapels, or abandoned churchyard sheds—wherever space permits a kneeler, small altar, and the Blessed Sacrament—many priests throughout the world instinctually know that this time creates an intimacy not of this world. It's where a supernatural peace breathes over and consoles them. It's where Sacred Bread leavens their souls, sanctifies them, and lifts them into their days.

"Your Blood now runs in mine," St. Maximilian Kolbe said of the Blessed Sacrament. "Your Soul, Incarnate God, compenetrates mine."[14]

This romance, experienced by the martyr Kolbe and all priests who present themselves before this unfathomable immensity at Holy Hour, often involves a mystical exchange. The holy priest's only desire, at the heart of the colloquy, is to hand over his heart to the sacred one he adores: *I am totally yours.* But Jesus *really does* offer his Sacred Heart to the priest—almost as if He stood concretely before him in the early morning shadows, reaching gently into His own flesh, past His rib cage, and placing His own Divine Heart in the hollow of His shepherd's chest. So, the wise priest opens himself completely to receive this outward radiation of divinity. It's all he can do. Prayerful priests have learned that offering Christ the chamber of their own littleness becomes their greatest prayer—because it slowly begins to fill with the divine.

St. John Paul the Great famously fell into mystic trances before the Blessed Sacrament. St. Teresa of Calcutta relied on a daily Holy Hour to fortify her for a lifetime of relentless workdays—as do the many thousands of Missionaries of Charity who continue to follow her example. Sts. John Bosco, Padre Pio, Josemaría Escrivá, Maximilian Kolbe, Damien the Leper, Thérèse of Lisieux, and Bl. Pier Giorgio Frassati adored Jesus daily. St. Francis de Sales famously encouraged Catholics to visit Jesus in the Eucharist "one hundred thousand times a day."

When the storm of impropriety slammed the Church in 2018, a handful of local priests immediately arranged for emergency

---

[14] Jerzy Domański, *For the Life of the World: St. Maximilian and the Eucharist* (New Bedford, MA: Academy of the Immaculate, 1999), 82.

extended hours of Adoration to bring their flock back to a face-to-face intimacy with the heart of their Faith. Although these priests increased their litanies, held prayer services, and opened up forums to take hits from their parishioners on behalf of fallen priests, they knew that meditative time spent in the light of the Blessed Sacrament would best heal parishioners' hearts and reorient a confused Church. "Turn away from your revulsion," these priests seemed to suggest. "Look at Him now."

"People are wounded; they don't know who to turn to," said Fr. Dan Leary, who hosted a twenty-four-hour period of Adoration called "Day of Prayer: Repair My House" at St. Andrew Apostle parish in Silver Spring, Maryland. "The answer is, of course, to turn to the Lord. The Church has the best medicines for spiritual injuries. It's in the Blessed Sacrament where the ultimate healing and grace is."

It was rare for Tommy to go a single day without time spent in front of the Blessed Sacrament, where he became seized by Christ's Presence. One summer during college, Fr. Shaffer—then miles away from even considering the priesthood—answered phone calls at Tommy's parish. As one lazy summer day led to the next, the future Fr. Shaffer watched Tommy pass by the office each day to spend time at St. Mark's humble Adoration chapel.

"Here's this busy priest, always on the move doing something—but even on his off days I would see him walk past me into the chapel wearing a flannel and holding a Bible to spend time with Jesus in prayer," Fr. Shaffer said. "Like everyone else, I guess, he won me over with his big personality and his fun, but it was how he regarded prayer and the Eucharist that got me. He was always like, 'Hey bud, prayer is something ya' better spend serious time with every day. It's what all priests have to do. It's everything.'

"For him, I don't think his prayer in Adoration was some mystical or dramatic work. It was a disciplined daily decision to spend time trying to listen to what Jesus wanted to bring to him interiorly. And it was so easy to see that the Holy Spirit had spoken and moved him there, because you saw how he celebrated the Mass and the manner in which he preached. His prayer life is what made him so dynamic. At its root, I think the depth of his prayer is why people flocked to him."

Tommy, like other hardworking priests, understood that his toil was made simpler and more manageable by spending time in Adoration. He knew that every scandal, dilemma, or parish burden could eventually be worked out within that sacred silence. He could become fully available for the long list of names scrawled in his Day-Timer if he first made himself available to Christ in one of his several rectory chapels. Because he loved the Blessed Sacrament greatly, he was able to love people greatly.

Tommy certainly had many days when he wanted to skip his silent time with Christ, but he knew that his sanctification and his moral and spiritual discipline were nourished there. I imagine that his daily pilgrimage often came across as a penitential walk. "The spirit is willing, but the flesh is weak" (Mark 14:38). Without that sacred time, though, he knew that his ministry could be endangered by soul-rotting egotism. He also knew that his enthusiasm, quick wit, and large personality could destroy himself and his parishioners without the light of Christ to humble him—so he kept going back. He understood that time in front of the Blessed Sacrament kept his vocation from sterility.

Tommy wrote the following to his parishioners:

Mediocrity. I guess that is where I most see the remains of sin in my life. I am called to do so much; I give so little. Often I hear people speak about how much more they should be loving their spouses or children—and they are right. We all fall short; and often we fall short simply because we do not go beyond the acceptable or the minimum; we are mediocre. And really, is there any way out of it?

The "Yes" that is the answer to that question is one of the reasons why the Eucharist is the gift of the Catholic life.... To the extent that we open ourselves to the Eucharist, we become, as individuals and as a community, more than we are. We see our mediocrity—and we are right!—but God sees His people and works through us that we might become, in His Spirit, more of what He would have us be.[15]

A beleaguered, badgered, overburdened priest is often forced to stretch himself to keep his Holy Hour, causing pain similar to the creaking joints of an Iowa farmer who rises before sunrise each day to feed his livestock and tend to his crops. But it's within these unseen dry lands that the priest is able to make a heroic act of love: he offers himself as a victim for his parishioners. He knows that in this hidden form of intimacy, the priest saves and fortifies his priesthood.

I know of a priest who offers a Holy Hour for each family in his parish. For more than twenty years, each parishioner has received in the mail a small handwritten card announcing that his family—each member listed by name—was prayed for at a Holy Hour on a certain date. Some families have had their faith

---

[15] Msgr. Thomas Wells, "Antidote for Mediocrity," in *From the Pastor's Desk: Spiritual Reflections* (Washington, D.C.: Our Lady of Lourdes Parish, 2000), 85.

transformed due to this act. This priest believes it is this daily Holy Hour, perhaps more than anything else, that fortifies him for his role as guardian of his parishioners' souls. He's aware that many in his parish, neighborhood, and diocese seem off in a gully, on the side of the road, spiritually dying. They find the Church's revealed truths a nuisance and boring. Some Catholics reject the Church, fight it, desecrate it, cuss it, mock it, forget it, fall asleep on it—so this priest begs to become a mightier vessel to help carry them back. He says that the Holy Hour's divine sustenance steers and gives light to his entire vocational life. In Adoration, he believes that his heart, mind, and will enter a different dimension because they've been warmed by the furnace of the Divine.

In a similar vein, I have a priest friend who has missed only one Holy Hour in his fifteen years as a priest; his steadfastness might be because he discerned his vocation in front of a monstrance. Back when he was a stockbroker in Washington, D.C., he accepted the challenge of a friend and agreed to commit himself to forty successive days of Holy Hours. His first attempt with the friend was pitiful. He spent fifty minutes leafing through a missalette. The next day, everything changed. His friend suggested that he simply look with love at Jesus in the monstrance. No reading material. No rosary. No Scripture—just opening the doorway of his mind to meditative adoration. Thereafter, time stood still as a wall of love seemed to envelop him.

"I fell into a sort of deep devotion to Christ that day," the priest said. "My friend nudged me and told me it was time to go. And I was like, 'What are you talking about? We've only been here for ten minutes.' And he's like, 'Dude, we've been here for an hour and a half.'"

Thereafter, this future priest started pedaling his bike daily through every type of weather to be with Jesus at Holy Hour.

"That made it kind of cooler," he said. "I had to get through some tough parts of D.C. to get to Jesus. It felt kind of dangerous, like I was doing something extra for Him. But I later learned it was God who was doing something in me."

Now, years later, he knows that he's at war with Satan, so he comes to his Adoration chapel—a place he knows Satan cannot penetrate. Here, he prays for the destruction of spiritually dangerous strongholds, knowing that the world is full of prodigal sons reluctant to make their return to the faith. He prays for their homecoming—and that he'll be ready to embrace them when they come back. He understands that his vocation is without soul and muscle unless he perseveres for his flock in Adoration, so he offers himself as a victim for Jesus to help heal his parishioners' white-collar humiliations, abandonments, repeated sins, and other hidden agonies.

Nearly half of his parishioners have been born into a heavily commercialized age, in which they've been led to adore themselves rather than Christ. He says it's a sad realization that many would not even conceive of adoring Jesus in the Eucharist, even for a few minutes. So, in a sense, he makes up for their absence— and in a very real way, a certain shamefaced population of his parish rely on this hero-sluggard dynamic. They know he's a priest who adores the Blessed Sacrament and who is willing to fight for their souls, even when they're not putting up much of a fight themselves. He's on his knees when they're in the Redskins luxury suite. He begs as they dine. He listens to Christ's voice in silence as his overscheduled flock moves frantically from one thing to the next. The sanctuary lamp flickers as the glow of a flat screen engulfs every family room in the neighborhood. But they are his flock—and he cares for them by giving himself to them, a warm current of sacrificial, unseen love.

The Priests We Need to Save the Church

There's a feeling akin to the midnight friendlessness of Gethsemane here; obedience leads this priest to plead before a voiceless God to hearten his beloved, sleepy-eyed flock. He is their shepherd, who has assumed a share in the identity of the Man of Sorrows (see Isa. 53:1–6). Here, he begs to be saturated with the graces of Christ — and that has been the secret of his commitment to his Holy Hour. He has found the strength of his Father in the heart of the hour-long sacrifice. It has enabled him to hand himself over as a victim for the parishioners he has vowed to love and guide.

A parish aware that its shepherd places himself daily in the presence of the Blessed Sacrament is a parish at peace. Open-eyed parishioners treasure the time their pastor has set aside to spend at Holy Hours because they innately know he's protecting them. The bridegroom protects his Bride — the church and the souls within — with a chivalric, mannerly offering of sacrificial love. The holier the priest becomes, the holier is his parish.

At the heart of this hour is an intense hunger for perfect union with God. This desire to know God more fully so that he might feed His lambs more fully burns within the priest. Beautifully, the manner of his tender care for his parishioners' souls has become as intentional as his care for his own soul. In a way, he figures, if their souls are damned, he played a part in it. And he might one day be joining them.

"They need to know that as their pastor, I'm praying for them in that chapel, and I care deeply for their souls," the former stockbroker said. "These families probably ought to know that their pastor will never abandon them, that I'll always have their backs in prayer — and that I'll do my best to care for every soul in their families."

This priest is simply obliging his Father's wishes.

If you'll pardon one more baseball intrusion, I'd like to bring Cal back for something I believe is significant. On the night the future Oriole was born, his father, Cal Ripken Sr., was an eighteen-hour drive away in Topeka, Kansas, playing in a meaningless and forgotten minor league baseball game. From his first breath, for better or worse (probably worse), the course of his son's life was molded: *Boy, this is baseball, and it's an important game. I'll be back for you soon.* Cal Sr. was a leather-skinned, tough man who'd walk a mile just to block a wild pitch in the dirt. He smoked unfiltered cigarettes, drank Schlitz, and cussed, but he adored baseball—not the phony, poetic rendering of America's pastime, but the disciplined, working side of it. From the age of three, Cal received from his father his own strict but necessary interpretation of the game, coupled with a pair of unbending principles: abide by the game's fundamentals, and oblige them always. Practice didn't make perfect, he famously said; *perfect* practice made perfect. *Never abandon the fundamentals* was the eternal echo of Cal Jr.'s childhood. The fruits of an unwavering and disciplined approach, Cal Sr. said, would pay off with a rich harvest.

Simply put, Cal's love for his vocation stemmed directly from two elements: his obstinate allegiance to his duty and the love and guidance of his father. Not only did he attempt to imitate all he learned from his dad, but it seemed as if he was giving himself back to his father, even if he had to carry a cross of physical pain to do so. Former Orioles coach Elrod Hendricks once told me that Cal relied on remarkably vast reservoirs of stamina and resolve just to show up at the ballpark. "There were days when Cal walked in limping, and I told myself there was no way he was going to play. He was in agony," he said. "But he put on that uniform and trotted out to third base. No matter what, he was going to play."

Cal once told me: "I always molded myself, my approach to the game, my values, my work ethic after my dad. I will always work off that base."

St. Margaret Mary Alacoque said that, in a vision, Christ expressed to her His lament at feeling abandoned by His shepherds. "I have a burning thirst to be honored in the Blessed Sacrament, and I find hardly anyone who endeavors according to my desires to quench that thirst by making some returns to me," the saint said He told her.[16] In the popular book *In Sinu Jesu: When Heart Speaks to Heart — The Journal of a Priest at Prayer*, written by an anonymous Benedictine monk on the interior voice of Christ he hears at Eucharistic Adoration, Jesus spills His broken heart to the monk about the countless priests whom He loves, but who have abandoned Him in abandoning the Holy Hour.

The unseen shortcuts a priest takes cuts his parishioners to the heart; some are omissions that come under the pain of mortal sin. But perhaps nothing cuts deeper than when a priest rejects spending time with Christ in the Blessed Sacrament — because, in turn, they're never led to truly identifying the Eucharist as the pure fountainhead of the Faith and their vocation. And without a full experience of the saving power of the Eucharist, a priest's flock might rely on being fed by entrance songs, soon-forgotten homilies, coffee-and-donut fellowship, social activities, or a make-me-feel-good worldly parish outreach divorced from the true source of joy. I've found that many in this population often wind up in the nondenominational church down the road.

Perhaps, then, it's no coincidence that because many priests have jettisoned the Holy Hour — and have stopped proposing its fruits to their flock — so many Catholics lack fervent prayer lives

---

16 Sheen, *The Priest Is Not His Own*, 89.

or even of a belief in the Real Presence of Jesus in the Eucharist. The measure of a priest, it would seem, is his awed reverence for the Blessed Sacrament. It maps his entire vocation.

Cal Ripken is enshrined at the Baseball Hall of Fame in Cooperstown, New York, with other players celebrated for their work ethic — Ty Cobb, Lou Gehrig, Jackie Robinson, and Roberto Clemente, to name a few. Although I imagine that these players and their discipline pleased God, these traits were not rendered for God. I suspect that these athletes were in it to make a good living, have fun, and win games.

I imagine what a priest would resemble if he displayed the grind-it-out trait of Cal and these luminaries — and what enshrinement would await him. I imagine how such a priest would be greeted in heaven: by a long line of saints whose souls he had once touched.

I imagine that this priest, if you penetrated his core, would be someone who'd built his life on the foundation of the Eucharist.

Near the end of his life, Archbishop Sheen's resoundingly heroic life and mission gradually developed into a single, inexorable plea to priests: "Father, pledge yourself to the daily Holy Hour."

"The house of the priest is not the rectory. He is at home only where Christ is present," Sheen wrote. "There alone he learns the secret of love."[17]

---

[17] Ibid., 91.

7

Our Blessed Mother

I was raised in a home with a mother who desired sainthood, but unless I was paying attention, I didn't notice. I'm remembering now, for what it's worth, that I don't recall her ever purchasing an item of clothing for herself. She loved the Catholic Faith of her childhood, her priests, her family, and jigsaw puzzles; that's about it. And wouldn't you know it, right after the last of her eight children, John, left home, Judy Wells died too young from cancer.

If a single snapshot is able to capture the image of a lifetime, it would be this of Mom: I would occasionally walk unannounced into my parents' bedroom to find her in the afternoon's half-light, kneeling alone by her bed, praying the Holy Rosary. She'd look up with hesitant eyes that told distinctly different stories: her self-consciousness at being caught in the raw nakedness of prayer, and her hope that I'd kneel beside her. That openhearted look hangs forever in my mind like a warm remembrance.

Mom was certainly as guileless and meek a person as I'll ever know, but her love for truth carried her to places most others don't venture. She knocked on neighbor's doors, asking fallen-away Catholics if they wanted to join her family for Sunday Mass. She hand-wrote tender, pleading letters to encourage shacking-up couples to separate and renew chaste relationships. She worked for decades as a counselor at Mary's Center, a tiny, poorly funded pregnancy center in a tough area of town, where she continually encouraged calloused women to cast their ringed eyes beyond the veil and into the bright hallelujah of their babies' tiny heartbeat. If walking the unseen sacrificial path of small daily trials marked the identity of her motherhood, it was the Rosary that kept pointing her back into those disregarded places.

More than two dozen priests processed down the aisle at Judy Wells's funeral, wanting to offer their gratitude for her esteem for their priesthood. I think these priests realized that Mom — like our Blessed Mother — expected only heroism from them. In a stunning visual of Marian ferocity, Msgr. Esseff shared with me a mental picture of Mary as related to a priest's relentlessly heroic duty owed as an *alter Christus*; it was the same picture Mom could have given me. And after Msgr. Esseff shared this simple understanding of Mary, I have never considered her the same.

"Mary is relentless with me," he said. "Here's how I picture her: I see her on the ground taking me into her arms at the Fourth Station, and I'm already completely beat and broken." He paused as his voice broke and tears began to well up in his eyes. "And she looks at me and says, 'Your Father said, "You go and die." You better do that, son — you undo it. Please undo this now.' And she helps me up so I can move forward with the cross. That's who Mary is to my priesthood." His tears fell. "I can't be a priest without *this* relationship with Mary."

Throughout his many years of work with exorcisms, Msgr. Esseff has repeatedly witnessed demons revealing startling reactions, often horror, at the immensity of Mary's power. Due to this divine aid, he said, he has relied on her to drive his entire ministry of exorcism.

A priest friend told me a story of Mary that can only be understood on this supernatural level. At the start of Lent, he had decided to pray twenty decades of the Rosary—one for each of the Mysteries—daily. Two hundred and twelve Hail Marys every day until Easter morning. Then he came to realize that he appreciated the devotion to such a degree that he continued praying the twenty-decade Rosary daily. Sometime that summer, he recognized that a crisis had taken root in his parish at around the time he had made his Rosary pledge. Unbeknownst to him, a female parishioner had developed strong romantic feelings for him and had made plans to pursue a relationship. Inexplicably, though, her pursuit of this prayerful priest ended without his or anyone else's notice or intervention at the time.

"Tracing everything back, this thing started to surface at precisely the time I started [praying the twenty decades of the Rosary]," he said. "I believe it was Mary who was protecting me right from the start. This thing was dangerous, and Mary was steering it away without me even knowing. If I wasn't praying the Rosary, I really don't know if this thing would have been stopped. Mary protected me. She accomplished her work behind the scenes."

It's significant, I think, to mention two things I saw repeatedly while traveling to meet with the many priests who have helped shape this book.

1. Virtually every one of them had a crucifix—usually a rather large one—purposely affixed to a wall directly in view from his desk, a reminder to understand his priesthood in light of the Crucifixion and as a total offering of self.

2. An image of Mary holding the Christ Child or revealing her Immaculate Heart was close by.

The Priests We Need to Save the Church

Over time, I came to see these consistencies not as pleasant coincidences, but as hallmarks of a priest who intentionally pursues sanctity—transparent indications that the man I was seated across from was willing to suffer on the path to becoming a saint. Endearingly, this hardy confraternity of priests was entirely unaware of the charming thread that united them.

Presumably, the Church's shepherds would want concrete reminders of their mission by regularly looking to the bleeding Good Shepherd. And when these priests spoke of their devotion to the Good Shepherd, they spoke in the measured and uncomplicated tone one comes to expect from a serious-minded priest whose goal is to imitate the One he serves.

But when they spoke of the Mother of God, the atmosphere of the room seemed to change. Their visage, stature, and entire manner were transformed. Frequently, they sat straighter in their chairs. Whereas these priests had looked directly at me in sharing their thoughts, when asked about Mary, many stared at a fixed point in space. And when they spoke, the cadence of their sentences relaxed, and their tone softened as they adopted a tenderer and more lyrical rhythm. In a way, they had suddenly become like mystics holding tightly to Our Lady's hand, no longer speaking to me, but directly to her. During these moments, the actual presence of Mary was very strong in the room.

One of these priests fell silent for nearly a full minute as he contemplated his relationship with Mary. As the rectory clock ticked louder than Yankee Stadium, he submerged into a sea of private memory. Even his breathing slowed. When he finally gave voice to his thoughts, he said this: "Mary became my love. Then she gave me my priesthood.

"She was the one who pulled me out of the trash heap. After that, I was going to do whatever she said," remembers this priest, who is admired by others for the intensity of his prayer life. "The thought of being a priest was an absurdity to me. But in the watershed moment of my life, Mary told me, 'I know *you're* not the right material, but my Son is going to accomplish His priesthood through you.' That's when I knew I had to become a priest. Mary gave me an intimacy with her Son that I didn't think was possible."

In return, this priest surrendered his entire priesthood to Mary's care and her Immaculate Heart.

Although some might read this gesture as piously theatrical, it's hardly unique. St. Peter's Square couldn't contain the volume of priest saints and martyrs who, from the dawn of their formation, became determined to consecrate their lives to Jesus through Mary. The logic behind these Marian consecrations has an uncomplicated symmetry. From her first encounter, as a teenager, with heaven's divine messenger, Mary repeatedly responded with an unqualified yes to God's call. Truly heroic priests long to do the same out of obedience to their Mother. *Yes* is how properly trained priests long to serve God. *Yes* has become the breath of these priests' souls because they know it demands a certain acceptance of dying, as perhaps St. Joseph understood, too, as his God-chosen wife slept in the cold cave in Bethlehem.

The many Marian priests I met seemed to me a chivalric army seeking to conform themselves to Mary's sanctity and virtues. I came to see their stamina as messengers of God as remarkable, and their joy and eagerness to give of themselves as signatures of undeviating heroism, like knights of our Lady who kneel at altars for all-night vigils.

Tommy was intensely devoted to Mary; he placed his priesthood beneath her mantle. Wherever we traveled, he brought along a simply made, black rosary. I remember traveling alone with him on a four-hour car ride from a farmhouse near the small Irish riverside village of Garrykennedy to the home of his friends in the North. Moments after setting out, he reached for his rosary. "Let's go, Keggy. In the name of the Father and of the Son ..." My instinctual, internal groan begged that he shelve the rosary until we settled into the drive. His devotion revealed something nobler—he wanted his Mother to set the tone and accompany us as we traveled down narrow country roads. He continued to bring the mental landscapes of the Rosary into the remainder of our vacation.

He once wrote of Mary's single-mindedness, which explains why he never questioned the weight of the blizzard of obligations he awakened to each day. "The sorrows of Our Lady remind us that so often blessedness and suffering are connected. There is a certain brutal honesty in Christianity that cannot forget that blessedness means sharing in the life of Jesus and that sharing in His life means sharing in His cross," he wrote. "The poverty and humility of Mary at Bethlehem remind us of our attitude before the crèche. He did not need comfortable bedding; what He needed was faith, loyalty, and love. What He asks for is believers, like His Mother, who so believe in the Gospel that they will endure any suffering so that His name might be known and loved."[18]

I believe Tommy's "face-to-face" encounter with the Mysteries of the Rosary was the reason he was devoted to it. He visualized the hesitancy in Mary's eyes at the Annunciation, the shine of their joy when a fully pregnant Elizabeth greeted her, and their glowing furnace of expectation at Pentecost. Because his devotion to her was strong, I imagine that Tommy fell to his knees right

---

[18] Msgr. Thomas Wells, "Mary: The First and Perfect Disciple," in *From the Pastor's Desk*, 97.

beside Mary at her Son's scourging. In contemplating Mary in the Rosary, my uncle didn't regard her with softhearted sentimentality. For him, Mary seemed warlike, one who squared her shoulders and refused to look away from a multiheaded red dragon. She crushed the ancient serpent with the same calloused feet that stood beneath the horror of the cross. Tommy saw Mary as the queen and commander of heaven's angels, and he knew that St. Michael the Archangel bowed to her before engaging with the world of demons below.

Another Marian priest, who consistently works seventy-plus-hour weeks, says this of his Mediatrix: "From the beginning of my priesthood, Mary became an enormous presence. But right away, as my Mother, she made it known to me that she expected a lot out of me. Now, it's as if she sits on the sidelines of my priesthood and says to me, 'Hey, you're a priest my Son wants to become a saint. I know you can play better.' But at the same time, I know Mary has my back, and that has given me the strength I need as a priest."

The strong priest grasps Mary's spiritual motherhood because of what unfolded in the lonely shadow of the cross, when, between heaving breaths, her dying Son whispered that she protect His beloved apostle. At that moment—bloodstained, sickened, and seemingly forsaken—Mary hoisted the vocation of the priesthood upon her back. After lifting her eyes to receive her Son's final request, she cast them on the beloved apostle, John. It was then that a mystical, maternal dimension entered the priesthood: Mary became its safeguard. In Mary's perfect obedience at the foot of the cross, she began to shape the souls of the many millions of her Son's future priests.

Priests know the daunting truth that they represent John, due to Christ's final request that he protect His Mother. Over time, this call has stirred the hearts of many holy priests to make themselves slaves to Jesus *through Mary*. This profound act of submission unlocks two Marian promises: that she will be present in their work for her Son, and that she will maintain a motherly solicitude for their duties. She's the Mother who helps to keep the son's conduct aboveboard, well oiled, and true. An obedient son never wants to disappoint his mother—especially when she is also Mother of his soul. One would imagine that beloved John felt a strong pull toward meritorious behavior after taking Mary into His home.

Marian priests seem to offer a free hand to Our Lady; they are of one mind in accepting indignities, desolation, and exhaustion—the very feelings Mary endured as she stood immovably beneath the cross. Because they've entrusted themselves to her, their offer of self-denial becomes a harmonious participation in the self-offering of Christ, whose lifeless body Mary held in her lap. They surrender all aspects of their ministry to her as an offering to her Son. All is for Mary. *In persona Christi*, they strive to conform themselves into the stone the builder rejected, but it's a Herculean task to chisel oneself into that stone—so they fly to their Mother for her succor.

As earthbound "free agents," priests experience human fragility over time (as does everyone), and this can diminish their obligation to mirror Christ's crucified life. By contemplating the fruit of Mary's virtues, though, priests are better able to imitate them. It is within that twofold action focused on Mary—meditation and imitation—that priests enter into an interior life that helps feed a heroic vocation in service to Christ.

"It's not important for a priest to have a relationship with Mary. It is *essential*. Devotion to her is not optional," said Msgr. Andrew Baker, the rector at bucolic Mount St. Mary's, one of

America's largest seminaries, at the base of the Catoctin Mountains in Emmitsburg, Maryland. He encourages each of his seminarians to pray the Rosary every day. "In the bridal relationship, she's the prototype for the Church. As a priest lays down his life for the Church, he should also lay down his life for her. Mary is the one who opens the door to the priest's heart and soul so he can receive her Son's graces.

"If a priest wants to be a saint, Mary is the sure and certain way to her Son. She helps us to live purity with great fervor, to pray more intensely, and to have a charitable heart. All of which she did perfectly. This is the path to heaven."

Tommy understood that to circumvent spiritual malaise and "rectory bachelorhood," he simply had to maintain a Marian dimension in his vocation. He knew Mary was a sinless contemplative who continually remained obedient despite severe trials, and even as the Mother of God, she thought of herself as nothing. It was within that awareness that my uncle found the perfect antidote to prevent pastoral pride, argumentativeness, withdrawal, and sliding into idleness. Mary was his perfect priestly model. No one else came close, so Tommy stood close to her each day of his priesthood. That's why devotion to Mary isn't simply one optional devotion among others. For many of the priests influenced by Tommy, Marian devotion means spending time each day pondering her suffering Immaculate Heart. If a priest's humility, prudence, and prayerfulness is visible daily, it is almost certainly thanks to Mary's influence.

Since Mary is the source of all grace, it seems as if priests would want to open themselves to her constant care to help shape their ministry. Tommy cautioned many who rejected or ignored this interior Mother-son relationship that they did so at the peril of their priesthood. As the unique bearer of her Son's sanctifying graces, Mary implores Jesus for the gifts of the Spirit to nourish, maintain, and vivify priests' souls.

"Mary is the coworker in our ministry," Msgr. Baker said. "I don't see how a priest could achieve the full fruitfulness of his priesthood without a daily Holy Hour and a daily Rosary."

The priest who seldom prays the Rosary or ponders Mary's Immaculate Heart makes the sometimes-fatal error of thinking he can walk defenseless into the world in the name of Christ and not be harmed. The priest who discards Mary permits a gulf to grow between the priest he is and the priest God wants him to become; his dismissal of Christ's Mother is an iconoclastic avoidance of his *own* possibility. Rather than choosing to engage in the trench warfare of striving for a priesthood of Marian virtue, some seem to have settled for a sterilized and more comfortable lifestyle as their priesthood's truest identity fades.

Tommy, though, was greatly encouraged by the growing number of younger priests who were receptive to Mary. "I need her feminine influence," said one of these young priests. "Whether it's saying the Rosary, looking to a portrait of her, or just pondering her life, I find that Mary has provided the tenderness and antidote that's brought out the soft side in my priesthood. I believe that the more I entrust my priesthood to her, the more fruitful my priesthood becomes."

Another priest, one with a strong devotion to Our Lady of Guadalupe, annually leads groups of parishioners to Mexico for retreats centered on intense prayer, many hours of Adoration, catechesis on Mary, visits to the grand cathedral for Mass, and, of course, a pilgrimage to Tepeyac Hill, the site of the apparition. They bunk at a cloistered convent at the base of the hill, where they join with the white-habited Immaculate Conception nuns in their daily routines. This priest, and several others like him who take pilgrims on the relatively short flight to visit Our Lady of Guadalupe, see their role as priests to lead their flocks closer to the heart of Mary.

"Every priest needs a woman in his life because I think there's a part of every man that wants to impress a woman," the priest said. "And it's interesting: I've found as a priest that the more I fell in love with Mary, the more I fell in love with Jesus and being a priest. She protects my entire priesthood. She helps me with temptations, all my weaknesses, and my flaws. She is completely without sin — and as my Mom, she wants me without sin, too."

Mary has been instrumental in fortifying this priest's ministry, and he's widely thought to have helped place many souls on the path to heaven. Accordingly, Satan despises him — especially because the enemy of human souls knows that this priest is devoted to the "new Eve," who crushed his head. But this dynamic is nothing new. For two thousand years, mystics, saints, martyrs, and holy priests have passed on personal stories of the powers of evil coming after them because they served Christ in imitation of His Mother.

Occasionally over the years, I've been asked how my seven siblings have remained faithful to Catholicism. My own answer is always the same: we were a family that prayed the Rosary. Mom and Dad knew that Mary's intercessory work would continually lead us to her Son and would remedy the occasional pains, sins, and tragedies that surfaced in the grayish-blue, four-bedroom colonial corner house in Bowie, Maryland. I have to imagine that if Mary didn't have an unbroken presence within our home, some of us would have drifted.

My own devotion to Mary has only grown stronger over the years.

As I type this sentence, I am looking out my office window at a stone grotto that houses a statue of Our Lady. Shortly after we moved into our home, I asked a mason to build the grotto to remind me daily of what occurred in the aftermath of my brain surgery, after Stackman and Tommy collaborated like spiritual surgeons to save my life.

A bottle of Lourdes water was in my hospital room during Fr. Stack's anointing. I found it a month later, buried in a cardboard box along with the Hallmark cards, crayon-drawn pictures, letters, and get-well mementoes I carted home when the hospital released me.

I unscrewed the cap for the first time and a strong fragrance of fresh roses filled the air. Initially, I didn't think much of it as I imagined that all Lourdes water either carried the scent of roses or contained additives to mimic the pleasant odor. For at least two months, the fragrance remained constant as my children anointed my head scar with the blessed water.

Months later, I met the woman who gave me the water. As a member of the Order of Malta, she annually travels to Lourdes to help the profoundly ill into the curing waters unearthed by St. Bernadette. Over the years, she has brought home dozens of gallons of the spring water that she offers as gifts to family, friends, and the infirm.

I thanked her for the holy water. Then I told her how much I appreciated its intense scent of roses. She looked confused.

"Kevin, Lourdes water is odorless," she said. "You've received a grace. Mary found you."

8

Prayer: A Priest's Connection to God

I once knew a middle-aged man who was dying in the middle of his living room. Aggressive brain cancer had rendered treatment obsolete, so his family agreed to set up hospice care at his home. He spent his final days splayed out on a bed as his teenage children and wife passed by throughout the day.

He was often trapped within a noncommunicative haze, and his wife had watched him move from a state of fearfulness to anger, and finally to depression. Because of the disease and the strong medication, his usual lighthearted manner and sunny personality occasionally turned spiteful and accusatory, helping to change what was once a warm home into what seemed a place cloaked in shadows. Due to the gloom, his children had grown ill at ease and a creeping detachment and discomfort with Dad began to take root. "Can you anoint this man?" I asked a priest with reluctance over the phone.

This priest lived at a parish ninety minutes away, but I called on him because he was the most prayerful priest I knew. A week earlier—in response to a request from Krista—he had driven out to pray over a seven-year-old girl born with a rare genetic disorder that left her in a comatose state. The girl's parents later related that their daughter's rigid body and periodic convulsions mysteriously softened and she fell into a sustained tranquil state the moment the priest laid hands on her body and began to pray over her.

I was hopeful that the dying man and his family could experience this same type of healing, but it would require another long drive for the priest, to visit a total stranger. Already busy as pastor of his parish and its small mission church in a different diocese, the priest sensed the reluctance in my request and laughed.

"Hey, Kevin, I'm a priest," he said. "These are the things I do."

He agreed to meet me at a halfway point, and I would drive the rest of the way. He emerged from his car, head down, in a flowing cassock. He carried a small kit and a Bible. His chest-length gray beard and grave countenance lent him the appearance of a desert monk.

After a quick exchange of greetings, I spoke. Midway through my second sentence — "Thanks again for doing this, Father. He's in a bed downstairs and the cancer has ..." — he cut me off with an unsmiling glance.

"I don't want to hear any of this. Please. I need to pray," he said with the resolve of a cardiac surgeon scrubbing in. He dropped his head into a posture of prayer and, sitting beside me like a monument of single-minded purpose, didn't utter a word for the remainder of the car ride. The car's turn-signal indicator sounded like periodic gunfire.

Upon our arrival, he walked into the house and went directly to the dying man. Within a minute or two, he began to sing the Ave Maria softly into his ear. Thereafter, the priest requested that his wife bring a crucifix, which he placed on the man's chest, gently wrapping his fingers around it. Then he started to pray aloud the Divine Mercy Chaplet, joined by a few members of the family. The dying man's eyes remained closed throughout.

Finally, approximately twenty minutes into the visit, the priest began to anoint the man's head, where the cancer had settled. Shortly into his anointing, the man, who had been sedentary throughout, abruptly opened his eyes, threw out his arm, and grabbed the priest's wrist. His startled wife responded by attempting to pull her husband's hand away, but the priest gently said, "No." He explained that anointings sometimes became physically painful. Her husband, he encouraged her, needed to endure it.

A minute later, the man emitted a startlingly loud exhaling sound, as if he were just freed from being trapped underwater. Because the guttural release was the only noise he had made up to that point, it made us all jump. Thereafter, the man trained his eyes on the priest. The haze behind his noncommunicative stare seemed to break apart and lift and suddenly became replaced by a soft glow. In a hauntingly beautiful phenomenon, he seemed to take upon himself the gentle facial manifestations of the priest, like a mirror image. A preternatural peace spread throughout the room. Family members were overcome with emotion, by this sudden unveiling of an angelic countenance.

Afterwards, sensing that a certain heavy disconsolateness had settled into the home, the priest blessed each room in the house with blessed salts and holy water.

On the drive back to his car, I shared my observations with the priest, and he told me that the man's full-throated exhale was common during his anointings. He called it the "final release" or the "final reconciliation, when the fear of dying, pain from past sins, anxiety and anger are finally let go, heaved out, and surrendered fully to God." A part of *my* life changed forever that day because of that statement. The priest, a former hermit who spends many hours of his day immersed in prayer and Scripture, had seemed to calibrate his capacity for healing by spending the long drive in a sustained state of prayerful mission for this unknown, suffering man. It became evident to me that the man's breathed-out "final reconciliation" simply would not have occurred without the divine gift of this priest's intense prayerfulness and specific prayers for him. No one could convince me that the noiseless, prayerful ride to the house didn't enable the dramatic metamorphosis that unfolded within it. The man later died in a peaceful state, in a peace-filled home.

This priest who had anointed him has built his entire ministry upon the foundation of a deep inner life of prayer. Before daybreak and into the lonely hours of the night, he fashions his soul into a continual outpouring of adoration, contemplation, and a mystic's love for God. At any given point throughout the day, he said that he finds his thoughts are with the Desert Fathers, St. Teresa of Avila, St. John of the Cross, St. John Vianney, the Blessed Mother, and several other mystic saints; he invokes their names repeatedly. He knows that any lapse in his prayer life, in his study of the Church Doctors, in his vigilance during lectio divina (holy reading), or in praying the Liturgy of the Hours would endanger his vocation and detract from the high sanctity of his identity. He has a monk's heart. As such, he connects his duty to grow in holiness with his duty to fall into long, intimate periods of mental prayer. Some have come to regard this priest as a mystic, but he considers his prayer simply as a response to a grace received, as a gift endowed by the Spirit for his mission to intercede with God to reach and save souls.

"Prayer is direct union with God, so prayer is indispensable for a priest. Everything for a priest flows from Christ's Sacred Heart—His wisdom, obedience and love," this priest said. "I've been pretty busy running a parish, but anyone can run a parish. I'm a priest, and that demands that I spend time with God. . . .

Sometimes, when I'm lucky, I get a good stretch of time away from the parish demands—where maybe a few hours of time set aside for prayer can go by in what seems like minutes. When I was a hermit, four or five hours of unbroken prayer unfolded in what seemed fifteen minutes."

I have a close friend who joined this priest once on a mission trip to the remote tropical countryside of Jamaica. There, the two worked with others to serve a community of profoundly physically and developmentally challenged adults and children. When they weren't with the residents or performing physical labor, this friend said she never once was able to enter the chapel without finding him in prayerful silence.

"His prayer seemed like it bordered the mystical," she said. "He seemed caught up in a sort of intensity or deeper form of prayer. Whether he was in the group working in the fields or alone in the chapel, his entire attitude seemed one of prayer. He was within God's presence throughout."

Tommy too, had an unshakable conviction that the intensity of his devotion to prayer would shape his priesthood. It was prayer that enabled him to persevere as a faithful, hardworking parish priest, but also that prayer had the potential to open up doors to less-understood, supernatural levels.

John and Sylvia Hill believe that their youngest son, Joey, was miraculously cured after a mysterious evening intervention by my uncle. For many months, teams of gastrointestinal doctors were unable to discover the reason for Joey's precipitous weight loss, infirmity, and persistent stabbing stomach pains. He had lost more than twenty pounds in the span of a year and could no longer keep food down. He spent most of his days bedridden and in intense pain. With no clear diagnosis, his parents felt helpless and isolated.

One evening, Tommy knocked on their front door—something he had never previously done in his several years' friendship with the Hills. He would come in through the back door, and Joey's father, John, a long-time D.C. police officer, and Tommy would settle into the warmth of the den at the conclusion of a long day.

"He'd kick off his shoes, find his favorite chair, and we'd just begin to relax," John said. "When his schedule was free after 9:00 p.m., he'd come over from St. Mark's [his parish across the street] and we'd watch a game or just enjoy each other's company. He became part of the family.

"Then I opened the front door that night, and I saw a look on his face I'd never seen. He had his collar on, and a Bible and a kit in his hand. He asked in kind of an odd way, 'Where's Joey?' It was late, and I was thinking, 'Of course he's in bed.' So he proceeds down the hallway without another word. An hour or so later, he comes back out and leaves with no goodbye."

Disturbed by the strange encounter and by Tommy's solemn mood, John proceeded into his son's darkened bedroom and asked Joey what he and Fr. Wells had been discussing. Joey said he had spent the time in prayer with him. Then he pointed to his dresser and a bottle of holy water. "Fr. Wells blessed me," he told his father.

The next morning, Joey emerged from his bedroom and ate a full breakfast, the first he had eaten for the better part of a year. He said he felt strong enough to attend his elementary school that day. He came home full of energy and smiling. He told his parents that he suffered no pain or tiredness throughout the school day.

He never did again.

"Sylvia and I have never questioned it; what happened that night was a miracle," said John, crying. "Tommy came to our house that night in a way I'd never seen him. He came to pray with Joey and to try to take the illness away. And he took it away."

Tommy had discovered the impact of prayer decades earlier when, in the chaos of the early-morning rush to first-period class at St. John's College High School in Washington, D.C., he daily detoured into an empty chapel on campus to pray. He once told me that he found it "strange" to pass by the chapel, which was conveniently situated by the school's front entrance, without stopping in to spend time in silence with Christ. "I remember thinking, and I know it wasn't good theology, but I thought, 'If that's God, I can't just walk by,' " he said.

Shortly thereafter, he began attending daily Mass. Today, in that same chapel is affixed a substantial three-dimensional bronze plaque with Tommy's visage, as a memorial to those many early mornings of prayer. Even then, as a lanky, precocious teenager in a cadet's uniform, he seemed to know the secret of the Desert Fathers: no true relationship with Christ was possible without seeking intimacy with him, forged through heartfelt prayer. He found that this depth of intimacy with Christ unfolded most gracefully in front of the silent tabernacle, where, even as a teenager, he knew to throw himself open to receive God's unseen presence. Later, as a priest, he wrote about that silence: "Many, especially if they have never tried to develop a serious life of prayer, find silence intimidating. There is a kind of fear that if I stop to listen for the Lord, I will hear nothing. Ultimately, in some small way, we must try the silence of the desert, where no human distraction stands between us and God."[19]

After Tommy was ordained, prayer became a paradox for him—like being pulled into the towering majesty of Chartres Cathedral but being asked to kneel on planks of hard oak. Prayer

---

[19] Msgr. Thomas Wells, "Achieving Strength in Our Weakness," in *From the Pastor's Desk*, 109.

was inviolable and sacred, but often strenuous and arid. In other words, he shared the same relationship with prayer as many of us do; it was work. He knew why certain saints suddenly levitated while at prayer; he just felt that he'd never be one of them. He told anyone who'd listen, "The reason I speak of prayer so often is because I am so poor at it!" His heart was rarely warmed by bonfires of consolation while praying; it was the whip at his back and ashes on his face—but his faith told him, and he accepted with all his heart, that God was present throughout every moment of his time in prayer. So he rooted himself in it.

He knew that, as a priest, he had taken on the burden of making prayer the luminous center of his identity—he had made the vow to pray—so he persevered and trudged on, despite the dryness, and strove to pour out to God what he could of his heart. He knew God was moving in him in ways he would never grasp, so, in spite of himself, he submerged himself into greater measures of prayer, like the slumping baseball player who blisters his hands with hundreds of extra swings to maintain his equilibrium. He had been taught that virtues could grow only in the soul of the person who prayed, so five times a day, every day, he stopped everything to find God in the Divine Office.

Throughout my life, on family vacations, I'd watch Tommy break away and depart to the seclusion of the corner of a room, a porch deck, a riverside, a picnic table, or any other number of isolated spots—where he'd fall into what seemed a place beyond the limits of time. As a child, I wasn't aware he was praying his Breviary, but I would eavesdrop on what I knew was both rare and real. Shortly after his time in prayer, on each day of these many vacations, he'd open his Mass kit and offer to celebrate Mass for anyone who was around. In a certain way, I recall the day feeling protected by this priest who had seemingly insulated us with a wall of his prayer and sacramental tranquility.

"I know his Mass kit was the first thing he packed for his vacations," Fr. Stack said. "He wouldn't let a day pass without celebrating the Mass. God couldn't have given me a better friend and funnier priest to be around, but that wasn't the best part of Tommy. The best part of Tommy was his devotion to God through prayer and his love for the Mass."

One of his former parishioners, Andrew Royals, became a priest due in large part to Tommy's prayerful witness. "We are frauds as priests if we don't pray," said Fr. Royals. "If we don't put in the hard work of serious prayer, we're just cheaters as priests. Fr. Wells understood this. He knew that serious prayer simply had to happen every day. So, whether I'm in the mood or not, I know I need to bring in serious moments of prayer throughout the day.

"There's something dreadful about being a priest," Fr. Royals continued. "There's this solemn responsibility I have to the parishioners of St. Joseph in Morganza [Maryland]. I know I can't just ingratiate myself to them with friendliness and smiles. Jesus is going to want to know if I was willing to lay down my life for them, if I gave the whole nine yards. I cannot hold back because He didn't hold back from me. It's prayer that guides me into the fullness of understanding this."

So serious is Fr. Royals about this devotedness to prayer that he has taken to sanctifying his day by praying his Breviary in Latin. Although he knows that this practice is at odds with modern ecclesial customs, the ever-smiling, tall, slender priest says that his movement toward praying the Liturgy of the Hours in the old language has helped eliminate any temptation of "mechanicalizing" the Office. When he lifts his heart and mind to God in Latin — and breathes in and breathes out psalms in the same fashion as his priestly forebears—he feels in a sense as if he's joining with yesterday's priests and eremitic monks in their holy, never-ending chorus.

"When I pray in Latin, I can hear myself joining with all those generations of my brothers of priests before me who prayed this way—St. John Vianney, St. Josemaría Escrivá, St. John Fisher, Pope St. Pius X. It's as if I don't want to let my brothers from the past down," he said. "If I want to pray the Office in the best, most prayerful way I can, Latin is the way. For me, it resurrects those priests from the past. And there's something very enchanting about that."

Due to the priest's obligation to pray the Divine Office each day, under pain of mortal sin, the Breviary may occasionally present itself as a thousand-pound weight. But I've been told that even when the priest pushes past his reluctance, it's often a struggle to pray the Office *well*. Priests say that it's within this battle for deep interior recollection that character is developed; the wise priest knows that any half-conscious prayer or half encounter with Christ in the Office is an abdication of his role—so he surrenders himself entirely to God in this prayerful place. The faithful priest knows that he must find a sacred union with God within the Breviary.

"Because the Breviary sets the priest up for the celebration of the Mass, I've got to take it seriously," Fr. Royals said. "It's similar to the way [Major League Baseball player] Bryce Harper would approach a fastball down the middle. He's either gonna take it for a ride or swing and miss. But if he prepares well in batting practice for that fastball, he's not gonna whiff. It's a good feeling for anyone knowing that they gave everything they could to prepare themselves for the big moment.

"It's the exact same for the priest when he prays the Breviary to prepare for the Mass. When I pray the Hours, I feel like I need to give him all of me to pray it well. And He wants all of me. Sometimes it's a battle to give Him everything, but it's certainly worth the fight."

Although Tommy knew that prayer involved *listening* to God, he told me he rarely heard Him in that setting. He said his parishioners often related that God had spoken to them in prayer. "Keggy, I wish I heard His voice that way," he said. "But I don't. I guess until I do, I'll keep praying." St. Josemaría Escrivá said: "Put your heart aside. Duty comes first, but when fulfilling your duty, put your heart into it. It helps."[20] This was Tommy's blueprint for prayer.

A close friend wrote him a letter expressing frustration over her dry, distracted prayer life. Tommy, an avid letter writer, wrote back: "Dear Denise, the fruit of prayer is virtue — becoming more like Christ — not feeling good. The greatest prayer ever offered was the cross — and it seems to have been offered amidst some pain and dryness. Keep it up; stop worrying about yourself and how you're doing with your prayer. It is at its purest, simply time given to God. Let Him use it as he deems best."

Tommy's devotion to mental prayer, despite many times of dryness, flowed into every aspect of his ministry. Its fruit was immeasurable, but it was most evident in his preaching and in the mountainous work of spiritual direction, in which he emphasized the intrinsic need for a devout, persistent prayer life. He said it was prayer alone that deflected the subtle movements of the Enemy and managed to sustain his entire ministry; his ministry would be dead, he said, without the union with God and spirit of trust that he discovered and developed in interior prayer.

---

[20] Josemaría Escrivá, *The Way*, in *The Way, Furrow, the Forge* (New York: Scepter, 2001), no. 162.

The Priests We Need to Save the Church

He often relied on a charming kind of trusting prayer in his unconventional hiring approach—a practice that today most would reject out of hand. Rather than relying on more traditional methods, such as advertising for and interviewing potential employees, Tommy allowed God to implement His own plan of providence to make the hire. Often over the years, he'd pull a parishioner off to the side, usually after Mass, and say in his disarming, amicable fashion: "You know, I've spent some time in prayer on this one—and God has led me to choose you to be our new director of CCD [or whatever other role]. What do you think?" As the confounded parishioner was often left speechless or mentally formulating an out, Tommy would quickly posit, "I'll tell you what: I've got a little bit of time to decide. Take it to prayer for a week. I know God will give you the right answer." More often than not, the person accepted the position. Considering modern society's implementation of search committees and layered interview processes, his administrative style seemed pulled from a manual of the feed-store proprietor in *Little House on the Prairie*.

In recognizing that his new employee had emerged entirely through prayer, he left "God's hire" completely alone to perform his or her job, trusting that the Spirit would strengthen and guide his new staff member. "I had absolutely no comfort level and no desire to work with teenagers in their faith formation," said Michele Sim, a former parishioner. "But I guess Fr. Wells thought I did. He brought [my husband, Mike, and me] on, gave us a [teaching manual], and left us completely alone to do our job. He let us develop our own abilities through the ministry and trusted that somehow we would grow in it. It all went back to his relationship with prayer. He trusted that God had already worked it out for us. He trusted that God worked everything out that way."

Because Tommy understood that life itself could often come across as a fight, he pressed newly married couples to develop their prayer lives with intentionality and genuineness. His "wedding homily" on the necessity of devoted prayer became renowned in the Washington, D.C., area:

> I beg you, I beg you, I beg you—get down on your knees each night as husband and wife and beg God to teach you how to love.... Then one day—pray tell ten, twenty, or even fifty years from now—you'll look back on this day that's so filled with love, and you'll say in amazement, "How little we actually knew of love on our wedding day."

So often had he said this at the hundreds of weddings he was asked to celebrate that he became *gently* mocked by his large extended family of Irish wit: "Tommy, I beg you, I beg you, I beg you to please come up with a different version of a wedding homily." But the joke is on us. I interviewed dozens of Tommy's old friends, and they related how his infamous wedding homily—the crescendo of which requested that the newlyweds kneel before a crucifix each night to learn what true love resembled—truly helped to solidify their married lives.

"It was such an out-of-the box homily to ask the newly married couple to kneel down at night and pray together in that intimate way," one affected woman said. "But Fr. Wells based it on sacrificial married love, which was something he urged newly married couples to pray to grow into. Gosh, it was a serious homily for a wedding—telling a just-married couple that they would have to sacrifice their lives to love each other well, but boy, it couldn't have been more beautiful because it was all about coming together in prayer."

9

Asceticism: The Soul-Stretching
Work of the Priest

It was eighteen degrees when I drove past lonely cornfields and poultry farms to the snowy downtown streets of Wilmington, Delaware. I was meeting up for coffee with my longtime friend Mark, who was eager to introduce me to his friend, the newly ordained priest from his parish a short walk away. Mark had told me about the priest's giftedness as a homilist and his joy, which had sparked renewal at his parish, and right away, the young priest's easy laugh and bright eyes were warming to my bones. We had just finished trading stories about our shared appreciation for Bohemia-born Saint John Neumann—the priest's patron saint, who had spent a portion of his ministry in Delaware—when he asked what I considered to be the most important quality for a priest today.

"Martyrdom," I said. To his credit, he didn't spit out his coffee or throw it at me—although my childhood friend may have wished he had stayed away all those years ago. The priest didn't know I had been meditating on his question for years. "Just walking through that door a few minutes ago with your collar on was, I think, a small white martyrdom," I said. "It showed you as unafraid and a sign of contradiction." For much of the next hour, we dove deep into a discussion of martyrdom and the ascetic life; in fact, during this time when the Church is beset by wolves from both within and outside the sheepfold, I decided to break things wide open.

When the priest asked what I meant by "martyrdom," words similar to this came out of my mouth: every good priest today should have within his soul an impulse to die — to himself, for his flock, and for God. Drawing on the life of this priest's often-lonely patron saint, John Neumann (with whom I was familiar from a book I had read), I mentioned that unless he was willing to offer himself as a slaughtered lamb to overcome today's powers of darkness, he was falling short as a priest. "It's what our hero, Neumann, did every day of his life," I said. My broadside didn't draw a thousand-yard stare, so with the Spirit's zeal, I kept going. If he was preaching timidly from the pulpit, I said as an example, he wasn't doing any favors for his parishioners, his pastor, or God. The priest suggested that his pastor preferred more temperate preaching. I replied, "What does that have to do with you?"

The coffee was getting cold, so the priest went back to his parish, and Mark and I went off to the Oyster House down the street to order fish sandwiches; despite the conversation we had just had, he didn't renounce our long friendship. The priest did contact me the following day to say that he respected my candor and that he had taken to prayer my thoughts on lived martyrdom and the daily practice of self-denial. He also didn't tell me that he hated people who pop off like me — so it was a win-win.

A stranger pushing the ascetic life on a (formerly) contented, coffee-drinking priest might come across as arrogant or discourteous.

But there's an unbroken line of lionhearted priest saints who embraced this heroic journey to union with God, and whose sacrificial actions have been captured in tall stacks of history books. Like Neumann, they knew that an uncomfortable promenade of self-immolations flattens the will and stretches the soul into perfect union with God. Some of history's greatest saints—John of the Cross, Francis, Ignatius of Loyola, John Vianney, Vincent de Paul, Jerome, and Josemaría Escrivá—taught that a life lived without embracing self-denial blocks union with God and the tranquility of order in the soul. Self-mortification, they said, offers the noblest technique to fight off hidden sin, concupiscent inclinations, sensuality, timidity, and pride—the very sins that have so scarred today's Church. This revolt against self, priest saints knew, brings the soul into synthesis with history's most perfect act of love: Jesus Christ nailed to a cross.

Grace, saints knew, intervenes and increases when a person makes the decision to "decrease" à la St. John the Baptist. "He who wishes to find Jesus should seek Him, not in the delights and pleasures of the world, but in mortification of the senses," St. Alphonsus Liguori said.[21]

The Church has always taught that rejecting the world, the flesh, and the Devil brings illumination of thought and a movement toward holiness. John of the Cross's poetic soul was opened up to write one of the Church's greatest works, *The Spiritual Canticle*, while he was jailed for nine months in a six-foot-by-ten-foot cell with a shoebox-size window high up in the wall. Amid severe deprivation—with little food, no change of clothing,

---

[21] "Mortification Quotes," *Catholic Reader* (blog), June 7, 2013, http://thecatholicreader.blogspot.com/2013/06/mortification-quotes.html.

and no camaraderie—his mind became illuminated with words that would eventually help him be declared a Church Doctor.[22]

Similarly, while contemplating the loss of his head during his solitary imprisonment in the Tower of London, St. Thomas More experienced an intimate union with Christ's desolation in the Garden. More's final, unfinished work, *The Sadness of Christ*, confronted the slumbering apostles who wanted to do good but couldn't because of their bodily desire to sleep. Because the disciples failed in prevailing over their weariness, Christ suffered His spiritual warfare alone. Thomas More compared the apostles and Judas's betrayal to those in the corrupt sixteenth-century Church who chose sensuality and safety rather than rejection of the world and the flesh. The devoted Catholic husband, father, and uncompromising lawyer and judge knew what all of England seemed to forget: it was only through a graceful submission to truth and a detachment from self and material things that peace could enter the soul—even if that peace eventually came at the cost of giving his head to King Henry VIII. Thomas More died a martyr, sadly aware that Catholic bishops and priests had parted with that measure of peace.

"When the shepherd is lazy, the sheep are hungry; when he sleeps, they are lost; when he is corrupt, they grow sick; when he is unfaithful, they lose their judgment," Sheen said. "If the shepherd is not willing to be a victim for his sheep, the wolves come and devour them."[23]

In beholding the priestly landscape for the past several years, I've perceived what seems an unwillingness in shepherds to

---

[22] *John of the Cross: Selected Writings*, ed. Kieran Kavanaugh, O.C.D. (New York: Paulist, 1987), 117.

[23] Sheen, *The Priest Is Not His Own*, 118.

assume their role of being the "slaughtered lamb" (Rev. 5:6). Because judgment of others is perilous to my soul, I'll only connect dots. Seldom in the past twenty years of attending Mass have I seen priests even flirt with the idea of encouraging me to embrace daily mortifications in order to strengthen my pursuit of virtue. This is troubling, considering that the eschatological result of my slack spiritual life (i.e., the deadly sin of sloth) is likely my damnation, as Jesus reminded His disciples: "Enter through the narrow gate; for the gate is wide and the road broad that leads to destruction, and those who enter through it are many. How narrow the gate and constricted the road that leads to life. And those who find it are few" (Matt 7:13–14).

The deadly serpent of my pride coils itself within each dark corner of my life. Mastering it and the other obstacles in my soul should be the burden—sweet or unsweet—of my life. When priests fail to encourage the souls in their care to embrace the ascetical life, I can't help but wonder if they consider it to be important in their own lives. Or has this noble and purposeful lifestyle quietly become a Catholic museum piece, like hair shirts and knotted flagrums? Martyrs, monks, mystics, and Jesus Himself—"If anyone wishes to come after me, he must deny himself and take up his cross daily" (Luke 9:23)—teach the purgative way as *the method* of attaining the special graces needed to asphyxiate sin and dark habits, and to place strangleholds on our unruly wills. The practice of penance was Our Lady's central message to the children at Fatima, but when the hundred-year anniversary of the apparitions arrived on October 13, 2017, celebrations marking the miraculous occurrence were lacking in the Church; perhaps the diminishment was due to Our Lady's emphasis on the urgent need for penance. And I wonder how many of the priests who did recognize the Fatima centennial repeated her plea for the daily recitation of the Rosary. Did any of them speak of Our Lady granting the children a shocking vision of hell?

"Unfortunately," one priest told me, "the basic mentality of today's Catholic often seems to be, 'What's the least I can do to get into heaven?' And a lot of that is due to priests' no longer preaching on the need for asceticism and increased prayer. And maybe the ongoing attitude of priests who ignore asceticism is, 'What's the least I can do to save souls?'

"Sacrifice and self-denial are important for every Christian, but for a priest, they are far more so. It's very clear; a priest knows that St. Paul's message in Hebrews is of making himself a sacrifice for others' sanctity. It's his own ongoing spirit of penance that helps him become that living sacrifice for his flock."

This priest said that he has incorporated self-denial and self-sacrificial work into each day of his life to help snap the neck of evil desires, any form of spiritual, intellectual, or prayerful sloth, and to keep him mindful of his inescapable Via Dolorosa walk with his tortured Savior. On the day I spoke with him, he was in the center of what seemed to me to be a flowerless bouquet of thorns. For a ninety-day span, he emptied himself. He took only cold showers, abstained from all Internet and cell phone use (outside of work), rejected sugar, alcohol, movies, music, television (including sports), and any food in between meals. He also exercised for thirty minutes daily, supplemented his prayer life, and freed up additional time to engage in various works of charity. It's fair to ask, though: Did these restraints, denials, and practices help drive this priest to holiness?

"The odd thing about the ascetic life is that it makes the priest far more joyful. His self-denials ignite a change toward a greater pursuit of holiness in his priesthood. When the priest is streamlined, he's not a zombie. He's fully alive," the priest explained.

"On the flip side, an immersion in the sensual life for a priest becomes boring. It never satisfies and stunts the true growth of his vocation—and that damages the souls of his parish.

"A spirit of asceticism opens a vacuum for the Holy Spirit. It should lead me and every priest directly to the sacrifice of Christ on the cross; but if a priest isn't suffering, there's a chance that he won't be led to consider all that unfolded on the Cross," he said. "The ascetic life isn't a lot of fun; it's hard. It's a labor of love in which I need to partake. It sets the table for me to take seriously my only real role as a priest: to lead souls to heaven."

He continued, "One of the biggest problems in our culture today—and it's affected so many priests—is an overall lack of willpower. Just look at the many abuses in the priesthood today: the uncontrolled lust of priests, overeating, and alcoholism. But when a priest disciplines himself each day, he suddenly finds himself with more time for God. He's more generous with his time and more charitable and available for his parishioners. He has more time to devote to prayer. All of a sudden he finds he has that one hour each day for a Holy Hour."

I often think of the manner in which Jesus regarded His cousin John the Baptist, who launched out to proclaim Him as Savior. "Amen, I say to you, among those born of women there has been none greater than John the Baptist" (Matt. 11:11). Jesus, of course, realized the withering conditions and loneliness of John's living arrangements. He knew that His cousin, in part, had chosen to make the desert his home to subdue his flesh. He also knew that John's voice grew in potency and wisdom from the merciless habitat he had willingly chosen—just as Jesus Himself chose to enter the remoteness of the desert to steel Himself for His public ministry.

Msgr. Andrew Baker said that it's indispensable that his millennial seminarians grasp the value of daily self-denial and unseen sacrifices, especially in this age that lusts for sense stimulation. "Parishioners should see their priests as signs of contradiction; they must see them willing to carry the cross," Msgr. Baker said. "However, the value of mortification is simply not emphasized enough for priests, and mortifications are needed now more than ever. There are so many things we have to mortify in ourselves to become the priests God has willed that we become. We need to go to the cross. If Christ is going to live within us, we need to live the cross.

"Whatever it might be, a priest should have regular penances in his life that he and his spiritual director have discussed—a mortification at each meal, a stone in each shoe, no snooze button, no cell phone use. Just something," Msgr. Baker said. "The heart of the Mass is the suffering of Jesus; if we as priests don't suffer well, we begin to lose the meaning of Jesus' suffering. The cross can be the gold mine of a priest's life—and his parishioners will see that in him."

Over the years, I've noticed that the priests who took hold of conditioning themselves to surpass themselves were the ones who drove me more closely to Christ and who inspired in me a consideration of what was necessary to win the epic battle over my sin. There's something heroic about the priest who detracts from himself to stand guard by the souls of his parishioners. He has abandoned everything he loves for God's sake. He knows that he was made for sacrifice. He abstains from food for the entirety of weekend retreats, offering his hunger in exchange for retreatants' spiritual growth. He understands that fasting gives him power over the unseen world, as Jesus addressed in Mark 29. He keeps his cell phone on his bedside table, accepting that his sleep might be disturbed in the lonely hours of the night if he has to attend to an emergency. He rises daily from sleep in darkness, lights a candle, and falls into sustained prayer until sunlight filters in.

Other sacrificial priests have made themselves accustomed to kneeling on hard floors for prayer, eating smaller meals, and depriving themselves of sleep—all as expiatory offerings to help pull in wayward sinners. These are the priests who observe sixteen-hour workdays and would feel shame if they didn't. Jesus asked, "Can you drink the cup that I am going to drink?" (Matt. 20:22). Because these men of God understand that their identity as a priest comes with a price, they've developed a certain fondness for their penances, fasts, and voluntary renunciations; God has allowed them the privilege of witnessing the fruit of such mortifications. Accordingly, they've repeatedly seen their self-denial restore and (perhaps) even save souls.

At the break of dawn one weekday morning, four friends and I brought a troubled friend to a priest known for his vibrant spirit of asceticism. After celebrating a private Mass for him, the priest began to speak openly with the troubled man, asking if he appreciated his friends' help in promoting the healing of his addictions through prayer and fellowship. "Yes, Father, of course I do," he said.

"You know they had to find a way to work around their jobs and appointments to get here this morning?" the priest asked. "They must really think the world of you, right?"

Then the priest turned his attention to the five of us. "How much do you *truly* like your friend? How much do you *really* want to help him become healed?" he asked us. "So much that you'd be willing to fast for him?"

We looked at each other and coughed out a few gun-shy "Uh, okays." But this priest was unambiguous in his request. "Are you willing to sacrifice for your friend?" he asked. "Or was this ride out here this morning just for a private Mass?" We said we were willing to take up a fast.

The priest smiled. "Sounds good. How about we start a forty-eight-hour bread-and-water fast for him right now?"

We left the church parking lot in separate cars, wide-eyed and wondering. Forty-eight hours later, though, each of us had managed to hold the demands of the fast. And we saw the brutal harmony in it. So thereafter, we each agreed to incorporate a Wednesday fast into our lives, and to this day we've maintained the "no food" fast until we're at home with our families for dinner. Many other men have joined in. As time moved on, we incorporated into our lives cold showers during Advent and Lent, pillowless sleeping, kneeler-less prayer, and days, weeks, or even months without television, radio, and Internet. We've agreed to read daily from Scripture, segmented five prayer times into each day, and mandated intentional acts of sacrificial love for and additional time spent with each member of our families. We've committed ourselves to more physical exercise and longer time in Adoration. We've made attempts to attend a few extra weekday Masses. We've said decades of Rosaries in bank lines, on sports sidelines, and in traffic jams. We've made concerted efforts to return provocations, frustrations, and sorrows with charity and patience. Our lives have all changed to some degree.

One priest led us to this place.

All of the aforementioned practices may come across to some as mechanical, force-fed, or even, at some insidious level, self-gratifying, but to a man, each of us discovered that our Lents and Advents have taken on greater meaning, as if a secondary pilot light had been lit within us. It bears repeating: one priest led us there. Before we peeled from his rectory parking lot that morning, he mentioned something I haven't forgotten: "Sacrifice isn't a side job. It marks the mission and identity of a man." He added that Jesus had a really hard time with weak men.

A few years after our encounter with this priest, when the Church scandals tore into the consciousness of his parishioners, he decided to begin sleeping on the floor. To avoid the temptation of crawling back onto the comfort of his mattress, he got rid of his bed altogether. To this day, his mattress is his bedroom floor. This voluntary privation is a simple, unseen offering to help save the Mystical Body of Christ, the Church. Sin-tainted McCarrick and reputation-scarred Wuerl were both his former bosses; he suffered on the floor to pray for them and to ready himself to help his new archbishop, Wilton Gregory.

This priest preaches the gospel with conviction because he knows that anything short of it might leave his parishioners unconvinced. He addresses the reigning modern ideologies and the commandeering of long-held moral standards and exposes their dangers. As a consequence of his courageous voice, he has drawn the attention of hundreds of nonparishioners, who seek his spiritual direction, absolution, healing, anointing, and counsel for their troubled marriages, difficulties with children, and so forth, so the demands of his priesthood have been further stretched by those unfed by neighboring pastors and priests. His parishioners will tell you that he has built his entire vocation on an embrace of victimhood to help procure the salvation of souls. The priest would tell that you the hours of Christ's Passion are ever before him. What else could he do?

"If a priest doesn't bless his parishioners by accepting longer days and taking on parish inconveniences with a smile and warmth—well, he's not much of a father," this priest said. "A good dad will always have his sleep, dinner, or lunch interrupted to love his child well. Wouldn't a priest want to do the same for his children? Self-denial and an acceptance of the hard work of a priest lead him to becoming obedient to God and his role as a shepherd. How is he going to get to know the crucified Christ if he doesn't share in Christ's suffering?"

Another priest said that perhaps the gravest affliction in today's Church has been the unwillingness of priests to walk the purgative way and make reparations to help save the souls of their flocks. He said perhaps the two greatest indicators of this scarcity of self-sacrificing action are the lack of robust preaching and the meagerness of opportunities for confession. "The priest knows very well the addictions, the suffering of post-abortive women, the rocky marriages, teenagers off the rails, drugs, and pornography. All he has to do preach to the pains and open up the doors of mercy to relieve people of their sins," the priest said. "In a way, these actions of a priest are a self-denial. They're hard, but it's what a priest's been anointed for. It's his job.

"He might get blackballed for his hard messages, but priests have to be willing to take it on the chin to preach the fullness of the gospel. And that's a mortification in a sense, too. No priest wants to get lit up for preaching strongly on sin in specificity. It hurts. But a priest who preaches with charity and courage in regard to sin is the one who fosters conversions. His willingness to suffer indignities eventually bears fruit. The world might be hostile to his message, but something interiorly tells parishioners that it's truth—and it's then that the process of conversion begins."

Why does it seem as if so many priests have strayed from the living messages once sent by Polycarp, Ignatius of Antioch, Justin Martyr, Pope Fabian, Pope Sixtus II, and a sizable number of other priests who chose to offer their lives rather than to deviate from proclaiming the fullness of the gospel? These heroes were martyred for one reason: the Holy Spirit compelled them to extend, defend, and reveal Jesus Christ and the gospel to those who wanted it eliminated. They offered their lives because they knew that if they subtracted from the gospel, proclaimed something inconsistent with it, or dipped into the contradictory swamplands of subjectivity, they'd make heretics of themselves. So why have many priests today retreated from their mission to mortify themselves in preaching the gospel in all its fullness, no matter what blowback they might receive?

Fr. Michael Duesterhaus, a priest from the Diocese of Arlington, Virginia, offers some insight. He said that the trend toward softer homiletics and a decreased emphasis on self-denial is perfectly in line with modern priestly behaviors. "Our Church is dying, bleeding out," he said from his former parish in the foothills of Virginia's Shenandoah Mountains, "because too many priests have chosen against embracing a life of sacrifice and mortifications—so they don't ask it of their parishioners.

"When my brother priests don't see the urgency and need of sacrifice for their flock during these tough days, then the spirit of their mission is lost. It's a slow drift, where the priest's tepidity leads his parish into a lukewarm land, and the downfall inevitably comes. The parish looks like it's alive, but really it's dead."

The former USMC lieutenant commander and battlefield chaplain has anointed soldiers in wide-open killing fields. He traveled with his Mass kit throughout the Al-Anbar region of the Middle East, in Blackhawk and Osprey helicopters, in Zodiac boats over the Euphrates River, and in armored Humvees—all to celebrate more than a dozen Masses a week. His chapel's incense was perspiration, metallic sulfur, and burnt earth, and his choir's refrain was often artillery fire. His altar servers and lectors held loaded rifles. Roadside bombs upended four Humvees in which he was a passenger. As a consequence of his injuries and the effects of his three deployments in the mid-2000s, he feels as if he is "walking on burning coals every day." Doctors told him that both of his feet require amputation.

Fr. Duesterhaus didn't have the luxury of time to address the Church's deeper issues while serving souls in Fallujah and Ramadi. Now that he's stateside, he remains diligent to his duty to Jesus Christ and his vocation to serve Him, so he no longer minces words when he speaks of her shepherds. The bald, stocky priest said that the principal plague of today's lackluster approach lies in Matthew 25:25: "And so out of fear I went off and buried your talent in the ground."

"Many priests are throwing the gospel and the fullness of the faith in a hole and burying it," he said. "Because of this, their parishioners are walking around starving to death without even knowing it. And then you find a parish full of modern-day Pelagians and Arians. The Pelagians sort of figure good acts will get them to heaven, and the Arians will just kind of make up their own theologies and ideas to get there."

Fr. Duesterhaus said that priestly mortifications, more than any other practice, would resurrect the spirit of the priest and his parish and help lead souls to heaven. The action of the self-sacrificing priest, he said, provides the seedbed for the Church's regeneration. It's through a priest's daily self-renunciations that a gradual unfolding of graces rises within him. With those graces, he said, comes the uncommon courage and zeal to become a saint—which, in turn, drives his parishioners to desire the same.

"The bishops and priests who mortify themselves every day are the ones who continually create vocations. Because they feed the families at their parish, the families are healthy, and healthy families produce priests," he said. "Getting up at any hour of the night for the parishioner, skipping a meal, rising early each day to pray, *praying* the daily Office rather than *reading* it, praying aspirations throughout the day, in your car, on your walk to the car, wherever. Hearing more confessions, accepting to live in obscurity. Being Fr. Nobody — whatever it takes. A priest has got to have a plan for each day and a plan for his life if he wants to help his parishioners get to heaven.

"The priest who mortifies himself prays more fervently," Fr. Desuterhaus continued. "He takes his spiritual direction more seriously — maybe goes to confession twice a month. He's in the fight. And spiritual battle will come. But it's in that struggle in the spiritual realm and in the struggle for holiness that everything changes in his parish. His parishioners see that he's taking his fight for them seriously.

"But parishioners are smart. They also see the priest who has given up the fight, where they say to themselves, 'Oh, there's just no passion there. They've given up.' And the slide in the parish begins. There's an enormous difference between a celibate priest and a bachelor priest. We have too many bachelors in our rectories."

It's unlikely that the ancient rite of the sacrament of Holy Orders will undergo transformation — it's one of the Catholic Church's most hallowed and dramatic liturgies. But in light of the many scandals in the Church and the precipitous drop in vocations, if bishops did gather to discuss alterations or addendums to the centuries-old rite, perhaps they might consider inserting into it more reminders of asceticism and martyrdom and its meaning — perhaps beginning with Polycarp.

The eighty-six-year-old Turkish bishop Polycarp seemed to set the priestly standard in the year 108 when he was wheeled into a Roman arena to be set on fire. Eyewitnesses said a voice from the heavens could be overheard: "Be strong, Polycarp, and play the man."[24] Thought then to be the last man alive to have personally known one of Christ's apostles, Polycarp relied on heaven's instruction to embrace his martyrdom with both ferocity and grace. As the proconsul debated whether to burn him alive or set wild animals upon him, Polycarp said, "Eighty-six years have I been His [Christ's] servant, and He has done me no wrong.... But why do you delay? Come, do what you will."[25] He knew that the seeds of his martyrdom would hearten Christ's followers.

Martyrs inherit and take on the scandals, challenges, and issues unique to the generation in which they were born. St. Ignatius of Antioch inherited the challenge of Roman emperor Domitian wanting him dead, as well as the entire mushrooming band of Christians spreading the gospel throughout the Roman Empire at the beginning of the first century. Just days prior to Ignatius's mauling by wild animals, he wrote the following in a letter to the Romans:

> [Let] me to be eaten by the beasts, through whom I can attain God. I am God's wheat, and I am ground by the teeth of wild beasts that I may be found the pure bread of Christ. Rather entice the wild beasts that they may be my tomb, and leave no trace of my body, that when I fall asleep I be not burdensome to any. Then shall I be truly a disciple of Jesus Christ.... Only pray for me for strength, both inward and outward, that I may not merely speak,

---

[24] *The Martyrdom of Polycarp, or The Letter of the Smyrnaeans* 9, 1, Early Christian Writings, http://www.earlychristianwritings. com/text/polycarp-smyrnaeans.html.

[25] Ibid., 9, 3; 11, 2.

but also have the will; that I may not only be *called* a Christian, but may also be found to *be* one. (italics mine)[26]

"Woe to me if I should prove myself but a half-hearted soldier in the service of my thorn-crowned Captain," St. Fidelis of Sigmaringen said before he was martyred for his continued strong defense of the Catholic Faith in the face of revolts from Calvinists and Zwinglians.[27]

Take a look around. Blood doesn't run down America's streets. Emperor Domitian and the like have been held in check. For the most part, Catholics still are able to worship and to profess their Faith as they choose. They hold political offices and are CEOs of large companies, Supreme Court judges, and NFL quarterbacks. Their scapulars can dangle outside their apron as they butcher meat behind the counter, and it's unlikely that anyone will say a word about it. Things are rather comfortable, or at least the flesh is safe relative to earlier times. And yet within this comfortable setting, perhaps priests have found too-comfortable footing; many dread casting themselves in an unfavorable light or inviting alienation by driving folks to tougher standards of self-denial and holiness. But right outside their parish doors — right before our eyes — our children daily breathe in the zeitgeist, the "spirit of the age," in which zealous apostles of modernism have flipped reason and natural moral laws on their heads. The fight to advance this counter-religion of godlessness is as unrelenting as the heretical pushes for Gnosticism, Arianism, and Pelagianism.

---

[26] Fr. John Hardon S.J., "St. Ignatius of Antioch," Real Presence Association, http://www.therealpresence.org/archives/Saints/Saints_045.htm.

[27] "St. Fidelis of Sigmaringen," Catholic Saints Info, https://catholicsaints.info/saint-fidelis-of-sigmaringen/.

The Priests We Need to Save the Church

The strong priest pushes back. St. Ignatius Loyola spoke of the *agendo contra* (action against) that priests must undergo to imitate the humiliation of Christ. When a priest willingly acts contrary to his nature, selflessly accepting mortifications and renouncing worldliness, his actions directly reflect his desire to spill his blood as a salve to protect his flock and show Christ to the world. These continual sacrifices offer his most vivid testimony of crucified love. Jesuit martyrs Isaac Jogues, Jean de Brébeuf, and their companions bore out the *agendo contra* when they were tortured to death in North America a century after their order's founder, Ignatius, spoke about it.

As the Eternal High Priest, Christ suffered desolation, complete separation from God, torture, and finally death. In saving us in such a fashion, He offered priests the ultimate example of the chasm a shepherd must willingly cross to love and save his daughters and sons. "[Jesus] learned obedience from the things he suffered" (Heb. 5:8). Confronting sin and modernistic thought in today's culture stipulates that priests embrace sufferings similar to those embraced by Christ. It's this action that reveals his fullest identity with his Savior. Heroic virtue, stouthearted preaching, deep devotion to prayer, untiring charitable acts, and ascetic witness all mark the priest's share in Christ's cross.

Due to the manner of his death, Msgr. Thomas Wells is referred to by hundreds of folks in the Washington, D.C., area as a martyr. He'd be uncomfortable with the term and might give me a noogie if I even suggested it. But many believe that his true martyrdom was in living as a suffering servant, in the manner in which he continually received souls seeking his direction. He knew that passivity and lukewarmness didn't mark the shepherd, so he preached fearlessly, surrendered his time freely, and constantly sought to move individuals closer to living out the demands of their Faith. As a conduit of God's love, he knew his mission was to be their spiritual watchdog. His committed prayer life anchored his soul to that mission.

Two nights before his death, Tommy's entire message to Krista and me was to empty ourselves so Christ would live within us. In a sense, he requested that we die to many aspects of the people we'd spent our lives becoming. Tommy once wrote to a friend, "The Word sacrificed Himself for sinners, but the sinner sacrifices others for himself. But the cross is the ultimate norm of justice, and it is the place where the human person finds his deepest truth. Christ surrenders His entire self to the Father, and in this total exit-from-self, Christ recovers Himself in the Church, His Body."

The skin-and-bones of my identity as a husband and father is sacrifice. If I refuse to detach from myself—refuse to clean up the 3:00 a.m. vomit, to arise in darkness to pray for lovely Krista, to pick up Sean from basketball practice in the thick of the Beltway evening rush hour, to spend time fasting from food, or to subtract from my comforts to help ensure stability in my family—well, I'm a slothful, negligent, and rather disgraceful dad. That priests would embrace mortifications, penances, and inconveniences for the Church would seem to fall exactly in line with what my family should expect from me. I have to believe that residing in the hesitant priests' hearts is a desire to contend with the modern and changing culture. The priest knows that he's a sign of contradiction, and as such, he knows that a certain form of martyrdom and mortification is required. He knows that he must arm himself by fasts, prayer, and privations so that these continual onslaughts and heavy vocational demands might eventually seem like mere fleabites.

"The mortified priest, the priest detached from the world— these inspire, edify and Christify souls," Archbishop Sheen said.

"Being the father of many children requires work. Our Lord made his two greatest converts when he was tired. The eight-hour day, five-day week is not prescribed in the Scriptures."[28]

Throughout Vianney's long day of hearing confessions, he often ate only half a potato.

Padre Pio eventually began to anticipate and even look forward to nightly tortures from demons.

Anthony of the Desert slept in deep tombs and kept awake by praying throughout the night.

John Neumann, who died in the middle of a street while on an errand of charity, routinely traveled many miles alone on horseback throughout the wilds of western Pennsylvania to celebrate a Mass for a single household.

Damien of Molokai became a leper because he loved lepers and wouldn't abandon them.

John Paul the Great slept on hard floors.

Francis de Sales wore hair shirts and iron belts.

Addressing persistent assaults on moral law and confronting modernism's steady drumbeat is the martyrdom of today's priests. It will earn them their martyrs' crowns. And it will begin to steer their flocks—and maybe the world—back to grace.

Will today's priests play the man?

"Amen, amen I say to you, unless a grain of wheat falls to the ground and dies, it remains just a grain of wheat. But if it dies, it produces much fruit," Jesus said. "Whoever loves his life loses it, and whoever hates his life in this world will preserve it for eternal life" (John 12:24–25).

---

[28] Sheen, *The Priest Is Not His Own*, 132.

10

The Fatherhood of the Priest

Assumption Church rests like a small stone lighthouse in the jagged core of one of Washington, D.C.'s most imperiled neighborhoods. Waves of shootings, opioid overdoses, and assaults seem perpetually to threaten the narrow brick houses that cluster around the enduring Catholic church. But Fr. Greg Shaffer steps outside his rectory each morning to greet his community as a dynamo. His voice, he knows, must be a blazing contradiction to cut through bleakness and smooth the edges of worn-out souls.

On the wintry morning we spoke about the priesthood and Fr. Shaffer's long relationship with Tommy, the former high school baseball player stooped down, packed snow in his bare hands, and rifled a snowball at an unsuspecting parish staff member. A snowball fight ensued as wide-eyed, laughing children looked on. Fr. Shaffer challenges African American youth in his neighborhood to one-on-one pick-up basketball games as a means to gain potential new parishioners. "If I win, I'll see you at Mass on Sunday." His commitment to heralding the fullness of the Catholic Faith animates his devotion to the Real Presence of Jesus; he re-presents the sacramental value of the Eucharist in each and every homily: "It all points back to the Eucharist." His staked-out evangelization territory is the neighborhood around a

Metro stop, where he wears his collar and holds his Bible, spreading the Good News to folks who often just brush past, eyeballing him with suspicion and often contempt. "Hey man, a priest does what he's gotta do," he said to me.

Fr. Shaffer, though, has gained the full trust of his small church community because they've seen his robust and unmovable love for them. They sense what he knows: he's a father to their souls. His job, he says, is to safeguard his parish and help escort folks to the Kingdom of God. With this mission in mind, he decided in 2018 to grow his Assumption parish family by celebrating intimate Masses of healing, during which he lays hands on people one by one. Today, a wide section of his community identifies Fr. Shaffer primarily as a minister of anointing. Within months of beginning his new ministry, parishioners began to claim that miracles were happening.

"From the very beginning, Fr. Wells showed me that to be a priest was to be a father," Fr. Shaffer said. "I owe my priesthood to him. He was always there when I really needed someone—and trust me, there were times I really needed him to be there for me."

Thirteen years after my uncle's murder, a media storm suddenly rained down on Fr. Shaffer as he served as chaplain for George Washington (GW) University; he was begging daily for his mentor's intercession. A college student and active member of GW's Newman Center had become a vocal activist with a gay rights group on campus. He and another student, with whom he had been in a homosexual relationship, met with Fr. Greg one evening to discuss their activism. Perceiving their willingness to meet as an underlying hunger for meaning and direction, Fr. Shaffer spoke with paternal warmth about the Church's teaching on the complementarity of the sexes, quoting from Scripture and the *Catechism of the Catholic Church*, and gently unpacked their grave spiritual mistake of acting on their same-sex attraction. He then encouraged them to leave the gay lifestyle and activism, pointing to their need to live out heroic and chaste lives of celibacy.

But the young men didn't see it that way.

The private conversation soon became a citywide issue when the young men went on the attack, claiming that the GW chaplain's "anti-gay" and "anti-abortion" positions had "alienated" them and a cluster of other students. The college newspaper reported the students' irritation with Fr. Shaffer's "counseling sessions [in which he] advised students who are attracted to members of the same sex to remain celibate for the rest of their lives."[29] The two men said that Fr. Shaffer's counsel had drained them and had caused sleeplessness, anxiety, and loss of appetite. They called on the university to fire their former spiritual adviser; one of the young men had formerly served as a frequent altar server for Fr. Shaffer.

The issue caught fire in one of the world's most politically correct cities, and soon the blitzkrieg against the chaplain spilled onto the national stage. But Fr. Shaffer knew that the two students needed to grasp what a man of God does: he willingly enters the battle and protects by teaching men prudence, virtue, and self-discipline. So he remained undeterred and didn't give an inch to outside pressures. Although he had established a reputation among GW students as a "relatable, fun priest," he knew that "being one of the guys" wasn't his role. "I needed to be a father," he told me. Standing firm in the truth, he knew,

---

[29] John Quinn, "Fr. Greg Shaffer under Attack by Gay Students," *Courageous Priest*, April 2013, http://www.courageouspriest. com/?s=greg+shaffer&submit.x=0&submit.y=0.

was all that mattered. His ultimate job, in yearning to touch the suffering flesh of Christ in these two young men, was to be an unmovable shepherd who stood by the laws of human sexuality as taught by the Church for two thousand years.

"I can't say that time was a lot of fun, but in a certain sense, it really wasn't too difficult," Fr. Shaffer said. "I just did what Fr. Wells would have done. I just spent a lot of time in front of the Blessed Sacrament. That's where I knew I could find truth.

"I drew a lot of strength from Fr. Wells during that time. All he cared about was preaching truth, so that's what I tried to do. Another thing he taught me was that one of the greatest responsibilities for a priest is to guard his flock against sin. So when he preached and dealt with people's sin—he just went after it."

Fr. Shaffer considered each disparaging newspaper article, campus-wide condemnation, and personal anxious moment of darkness as a chance to carry the cross God had handed him. He was under no illusions: if he failed to pick up the cross each day and unite himself with Christ as testimony to the objective truths he vowed to profess—well, he wasn't much of a man, let alone a priest. So he kept sinking to his knees and begging the Holy Spirit to help him shoulder his cross well. He was also mindful of God's warning to Ezekiel:

> Son of man, I have appointed you a sentinel for the house of Israel. When you hear a word from my mouth, you shall warn them for me. If I say to the wicked, You shall surely die—and you do not warn them or speak out to dissuade the wicked from their evil conduct in order to save their lives—then they shall die for their sin, but I will hold you responsible for their blood. (Ezek. 3:17–18)

Hard teachings often bear a cost, but Fr. Shaffer slowly began to find himself warmly backed by an encouraging band of GW students, who offered Rosaries for him and compiled long, tender-hearted testimonials about his pastoral care — affirming that he loved them and that he often offered to celebrate two Masses a day, in addition to offering long hours of Adoration. They said their chaplain roamed the tony Foggy Bottom campus, where he'd drop his business cards with three words penned in on the back: "Call me anytime." The embattled priest also began to receive strong backing from a community of priests in the Maryland-D.C. area.

The media storm quieted and died off.

Fr. Shaffer's counsel and care for the same-sex-attracted men who met with him served a singular purpose: he was a father who cared for their souls, wanting to lead them to conversion. He knew that casting himself in an overly accompanying light could have facilitated the destruction of their souls and made a mockery of his vocation. He knew that his request that they pursue a chaste life was asking that they pick up and carry what could potentially become a lifelong cross. But he also knew that fifty-plus years of heroic self-surrender would do much to clear their pathway to heaven, where one day heaven's martyrs might hurry to embrace them, fully aware that they had chosen to die to themselves rather than being rocked to sleep by Satan's false lullaby of sin, permitted by a complicit priest. The peace that came from an ordered life, Tommy had taught him, was the utmost desire of the searching soul.

"For a pretty long while there, those two guys were my spiritual sons," the former chaplain said. "And I felt like I was their spiritual father, so I spoke to them as a father speaks to his sons. It's a sadness to me that it broke down in the way it did, but I knew my fatherhood to them was all that mattered."

Fr. Shaffer's constant prayers did bear some lasting fruit. "A year later, one of the men came back to apologize. He admitted that they made a lot of that stuff up and were heavily influenced by their new activist friends. He and I stay in touch a little bit now. We've grabbed coffee and shared a meal and laughed about it all a few times since. It meant a lot to this spiritual father to have one of his sons return."

Fr. Carter Griffin, the rector of St. John Paul II Seminary in Washington, D.C., has spent much of his priesthood studying and writing about the fatherhood of priests. He completed his doctorate in sacred theology with a dissertation based on the supernaturality of priestly fatherhood, and he published *Why Celibacy? Reclaiming the Fatherhood of the Priest* (Emmaus Press) in 2019. He believes that many of today's priests have abdicated their true paternal identity, which, in turn, has helped give rise to an orphaned and checked-out Catholic laity.

"Many priests view their own vocation as primarily one of activities in the service of charity," said Fr. Griffin. "While the priesthood certainly encompasses those, they no more capture the heart of the vocation than the activities of a natural father define him. A father's activities flow from who he is as father, as the generator of his children, as the one who's promised his life for their sake. When a natural father grasps this, then all the sacrifices and the self-gift take on a new light and make sense; love makes the sacrifice not only possible but even joyful."

Fr. Griffin continued, "Priests have, in many cases, forgotten this vocational call to be a 'father to souls' and, as a result, have reduced their own vocation to one of programs and pastoral activities. In this impoverished view of priesthood, both the priest and his people lose — he, because the joy of the priesthood ultimately finds itself only in fulfilling the priest's masculine ordering to paternity; and the people, because they receive the fruit of his ministry, but not always the fruit of his self-giving love."

Throughout Tommy's hundreds of grade school and high school classroom visits down the years, many thousands of youngsters experienced his crashing wave of love for them — as a father cheerfully loves his children. His guileless approach had at its root subterranean functionality: he knew that many of these children were not having their faith properly formed at home. His spiritual fatherhood, he understood, included a sort of hijacking of hearts and shaping of minds. He also knew that age-old truths and relics of the faith had myriad rivals — Atari game systems, the latest Madonna album, budding romances, boredom, teenage attitudes, that afternoon's basketball game. Because he still remembered when his own energies were scattered and his mind was distracted at that young age, his enthusiasm for the Faith came in full-throated fashion. He told comical stories from his childhood, belted out the Foundations' "Build Me Up, Buttercup" and made up ridiculous McDonald's jingles in order to loosen up the younger kids. Then he began the work of penetrating hearts by continually emphasizing Christ's boundless and unique love for each of them. His unmasked brand of joy was riveting and even startling to the kids. Many of them must have seen it as a reflection of what resided in his soul.

As his own father, Stanley, had done for him, once Tommy had gained their attention, he escorted their minds into the inerrant heritage of Church teachings he knew could one day save their souls. With a twinkle in his eye, he opened minds to ancient prayers and customs and to the Church's many martyrs and saints. He explained the significance of Christ's sacrifice on Calvary and of the unbroken line of magisterial Catholic teaching. He emphasized that the pursuit of virtue guaranteed a life of lasting peace. This readily available peace, he promised, only required striving for God by cooperating with the sanctifying graces given through the sacraments. The sacraments provided the fuel to make Christians into saints, he explained, because life-giving food would be continually poured into their bodies. If they took this form of spiritual nourishment seriously, they would become giants in the world. Eyes widened, ears opened, and hearts, in small or large measure, changed.

Because Tommy studied for the priesthood at a time when a destabilization of long-held Catholic thought and a reframing of moral codes had permeated many seminaries, he knew that he had to be a countervailing, fatherly presence to youngsters. He addressed the weight of sin head-on. Their Catholic faith, he told youngsters, was a supernatural gift given to them by Christ, and wasting it would have been reason for shame. He led them closer to Christ's Sacred Heart with a multifaceted teaching method that was an amalgamation of unflinching candor, un-bridled humor, and tenderness as intimate as a mother's caress. Occasionally, though, if headstrong kids rejected the message or simply had become a classroom distraction, he'd crack wide open stark teachings on the consequential reality of serious sin.

Back when I was in high school, I attended a retreat with fifty or so other hormone-fueled male and female teenagers from DeMatha Catholic and St. Elizabeth Ann Seton High Schools. Early in the morning, Tommy arrived to deliver a talk. Before he began, he called me off to the side of the large classroom. "Keggy, get ready for some fun today, budd-ddy!" He had that lethal, inimitable gleam in those Irish eyes that seemed to swim in even greater shades of blue during such moments. In short order, he began to expound on the Church's long-taught wisdom on proper courtship, premarital sex, masturbation, and other face-reddening topics—which he played like a kilted, well-rested bagpiper stepping into a St. Patrick's Day pub. He'd slip a sideways glance at me here and there throughout his address. "Told ya, Keggy," his merry eyes twinkled.

"In a strange way, because the sins of the flesh directly involve our passions and emotions due to the Fall, I imagine God might more easily forgive them," he offered. "But I'm not God, and I don't know! Premarital sex is serious sin and greatly damages our relationship with Him. I'm begging you now—don't even think about it! Let's talk about becoming victorious in virtue and walk another direction." As he maneuvered through the teeming jungle of his talk, the classroom walls seemed to be collapsing in on us as warmed, cringing faces began to study the checkerboard-tiled floor. Perhaps because he sensed he was losing his grip on his abashed, post-pubescent audience, he swung his talk into yet another direction, requesting that we imagine a seagull resting in the shade of the boardwalk in Ocean City, Maryland. When he told stories, his eyes blazed even brighter.

"So imagine this seagull comes out, picks up a single grain of sand, takes off across the ocean, and flies all the way to Europe, drops the piece of sand from his beak, then flies all the way back to Ocean City—only to get another single grain of sand and repeat it all over again," Tommy proposed. "This poor little seagull must do this for all 145 blocks of sandy beachfront. That's a whole lot of sand and time for that seagull, right? Really sore wings, right? I'm gonna guess it would take a couple of million years.

"Sounds about right, huh?

"Well, to a person caught up in a life of mortal sin, that would seem like the first day in hell."

The room went noiseless. Until the end of time, he told us teens, we are all caught up in a battle between God and Satan—"and, trust me, you don't want Satan winning." The eternal weight and gravity of mortal sin was real, Tommy said. Heroism would emerge, though, through a life of prayer, virtue, and enduring friendship with Christ.

This message clearly stuck with the gathered teens. To this day, some people who attended the retreat bring up the "seagull" story in my company.

Tommy knew a fragmentary teaching wasn't compatible with fruitful and true fatherhood, which he saw as his sacred duty as a priest. It was his job, he knew, to guard parishioners from evil and steer them from the tempting influences stemming from the allures of the world. He spoke and wrote plainly, as a father does. "The world will not be won to His truth and love by our conforming to its lies. Is the Church hated today? Of course it is, but so what?" he once wrote. "It is for us to joyfully and honestly try to live our faith in Jesus in the certain belief that the peace that comes from such living is the most attractive force there is in our angry and violent world."[30]

Each morning, when my uncle put on his collar, he saw himself as a representative of God the Father on earth, an adoptive father of his parishioners. He saw his care for individual souls as a trenchant commitment; he saw himself as an immovable foot soldier in the muddy trenches of lives. As their spiritual father, he maintained a profound sense of the office of the priesthood, and he knew that any deviation from judicious shepherding bore eternal weight. He knew that if paternal love was not tethered to truth, it was a false love. And because he knew that people could doom themselves to lives of sterility by choosing to neglect

[30] Msgr. Thomas Wells, *From the Pastor's Desk*, bulletin of Mother Seton Church, Germantown, Maryland, October 10, 1999.

God's fixed purpose for them, he fathered with intentionality. He directed many hundreds of souls in this fashion: after leading an individual into an awareness of his habitual sins and their causes, he tailored a unique blueprint for virtuous living. He then promised that if prayer and the sacraments were taken seriously, the person would eventually begin to find his soul joined with Christ's. Thereafter, he said, the person would find himself being conformed to Christ's image — and when that unfolded, he said, sainthood was possible.

"Right after he came, our parish [Mother Seton] became more Catholic. He made it more Eucharistic. His enthusiasm for souls broke us wide open to seeing the joy of the fullness of the Catholic Faith," said Deacon Bill Vita, who spent time with Tommy the day before his murder. "There seemed to be a missing spiritual component to our parish before he came. It was his love for the Eucharist, his love for the priesthood, and his love for people that helped mold us into a family. He became like a father to all of us."

As news of my uncle's murder swept into that wretched June morning, Deacon Vita was one of a brokenhearted army of Tommy's spiritual sons, whom he had helped form, guide, and teach. Some, like Deacon Vita, fell to their knees and wept. Others became like panicked boys who dart through heavy crowds to regain sight of their father. They abandoned their workplaces and raced their cars up Interstate 270, where they tried to break past yellow caution tape and remedy a remediless situation. Their father was dead. Brian Kane, Chris Starke, Rick Long, Tom Hibbs, Joe Patanella, Mike Mayhew, Matt McDarby, and hundreds of other gentlemen up and down the eastern seaboard of America found their sudden orphanhood incomprehensible.

"I never knew a man like him, and I never will again," said Rich Mulhare, who met Tommy as a teenager. "A day doesn't pass when I don't think of the impact he made on me. In a sense, he was my father. I loved my own dad as much as a son can—but my love for Fr. Wells may have been even stronger. He was the guide who steered my life."

Tom Sheehan, a police officer in 2000, was another one of those inconsolable "sons." He was the last person to see my uncle alive: he had joined three others to share an Italian meal with Tommy on the eve of his murder. Sheehan dropped him off at his rectory later that night. Tommy invited him in to hash out plans for the upcoming pilgrimage they had planned, hiking the Camino de Santiago in Spain with some others. But because he had an early start the following day, Sheehan declined.

As an officer of the law, he received a call to go back to the rectory and the murder site just hours later. "I've often thought over the years how things may have been different if I took him up on his invitation," he said.

"When I met him in the third grade, I instantly saw him as a man's man, a priest's priest. Everybody—*everybody*—was drawn to him because of his strength, but at the same time he was one of the happiest people I'd ever met," Sheehan said. "He was larger than life, but as a father, he wasn't afraid to keep me in check. He was solid. I wanted to be in his presence because he was solid. You felt safe sharing anything with him because you trusted him; he had wisdom. He was a confidant to so many guys because you could share with him things you wouldn't tell your own dad."

Fr. Brian Kane was one of the sons who hurried to the Mother Seton rectory the morning of Tommy's murder. "It's all I knew to do," he said. Two weeks prior, Tommy had flown out to Nebraska for Fr. Kane's ordination, and he preached the homily at his first Mass. When Fr. Kane arrived early at his new Midwestern parish to celebrate that first Mass, he saw a man in a corner of a side chapel, his head buried in prayer: Tommy. "Even then he was showing me what a priest does," Fr. Kane said.

"I heard the news, and I wept on the spot. My mind just kind of went on autopilot. I was in town, so I drove out [to the murder scene], got there, and didn't leave that day," Fr. Kane said. "I'm a priest today because of Fr. Wells. There was a time when he changed everything in my life. I was a suffering little kid, and he turned everything around."

Fr. Kane, the eldest of six boys, grew up with an undiagnosed learning disability. Because his first five years of school were an exercise in frustration, his parents, hopeful that a new environment would help him, transferred their son to St. Andrew the Apostle school up the road in Silver Spring, Maryland, where Tommy was the assistant pastor. Brian Kane knew no one.

"I was just a timid kid with no self-esteem," Fr. Kane said. "So Fr. Wells walks into the classroom the first week of school, immediately picks me out, gives the new guy this loud, warm welcome, and all of a sudden I'm validated in front of all these new classmates. It was the start of a blossoming for me. I think he knew I needed to feel love at that point, so he acted as a father does. He made a suffering kid feel pretty special."

A lifetime of friendship began at that moment.

"It was his joyful, fatherly presence. I saw it immediately, and it became contagious. I found myself wanting to be around him all the time because I sensed that what he had was real. His power and joy in being a priest became transformative for me."

The sixth-grader volunteered to become Tommy's altar server at daily and Sunday Masses. "I would have served every Mass that Fr. Wells celebrated if I could have," he said. As the years went by, Tommy led the youngster into a deeper love for Christ, the Eucharist, and the teachings of the Catholic Faith. As Brian's faith gained strength, his learning issues lessened. By his eighth-grade year, he was named student council president. He was admitted into Gonzaga High School, a distinguished school in the Washington, D.C., area.

One afternoon, just days before Brian departed for the University of Nebraska, Tommy took him out for a farewell pizza at his favorite restaurant, Ledo Pizza. At this point in their relationship, Tommy had instructed and nourished Brian in the Faith and had challenged and guided him. On this summer afternoon, though, the dynamic had changed. It wasn't like a father and son; it was two longtime friends sitting across from each other in an old leather-seated booth, awkwardly saying their goodbyes.

But Tommy saved the occasion for one last challenge.

"I'll never forget—it's the last I'm going to see of him for a long time. Lunch is over, and we're in the parking lot. He's opening his car door, and I'm opening mine, and he looks at me and says, 'Hey, Brian, you do plan on going into the seminary, right?'" Brian remembers. "He's got that smile on his face. That famous smile. The seminary was the furthest thing from my mind—until all of a sudden it no longer was. Someone I love and respect just floats this idea in my head. Then he drives off."

"Timid" Brian Kane eventually went on to serve two tours of duty in Iraq as a military chaplain. Today he is the dean of men at one of America's largest seminaries, St. Charles Borromeo in Pennsylvania, where he works at forming future priests into the mold of Msgr. Thomas Wells. Hanging on a wall of his office is a framed letter Tommy had written to him during his seminary days. Fr. Kane often removes the letter from the wall to share the power of its words with seminarians; it is written as a Father writes to his son. "Not only was every one of those words 100 percent true to help me live out my priesthood, but I've gone on to quote that letter countless times in homilies at weddings and Masses," Fr. Kane said. "The letter essentially states that priests need to be servants and men of prayer. And that's who he was as a priest—and that's who he was to me way back in the sixth grade. Whether consciously or subconsciously, I've tried to live out Fr. Wells's priesthood in my own priesthood. He was a priest who acted like my father."

As for me, my own father was never more so than when he attempted to infuse virtue into my mountain of precocious childhood habits. I still recall the crack of his knee on every other step he took on his slow climb up the stairs to deal with me after I was disobedient to my mom. As he stepped into my toy-soldier-wallpapered bedroom, closed the door, and walked past the beer can collection and heaping boxes of baseball cards, his face showed that he hadn't visited to be an accompanying friend. Filial piety certainly wasn't on my mind during these many visits. I did understand, though, that, as my father, he was the watchman and custodian of my soul. The need for me to oblige all the biblical mandates regarding respectful behavior were never discussed in these "meetings," but they were certainly imprinted upon me. As a father, he knew that sin needed to be beaten back, and virtue and obedience brought to the fore. Christ had introduced a "narrow way," and as long as I lived under Dad's roof, Dad would take it upon himself to see that I walked in it. He knew what I didn't: maintaining the path toward heaven enabled lasting peace.

When he gathered our growing family together to lead us in the family Rosary, or when he took us to daily Mass on early cold mornings in Lent, I imagine that he knew it was part of his duty to lead us down that narrow, unglamorous path of lived faith. When he arose each morning in darkness to get ready for work, he was simply doing what a father does to put food on the table and provide for Catholic school tuition for his eight children. He fasted and revealed in unspoken words that often it was our sufferings and sacrifices that brought us closest to Christ, while helping us to reflect on His broken body at Calvary.

A former army chaplain once sized me up and jolted my sensibilities: "Kevin, if you don't have a plan for your children to get to heaven, they probably won't get there." My dad got this. He didn't settle for a false peace with his children at the price of a haphazard or lazy fatherhood. He and Mom fashioned their identities around a fidelity to helping their children achieve a peace in knowing God; they planned it out and worked on it daily. If they could help it, together they would guard and hand down the richness and intimacy of this tradition, and as the years unfolded, a powerful symphony of Catholicism quietly played within us. All of their children are faithful Catholics today. Seven are married to Catholic spouses. One son, David, is married to the Church as an archdiocesan priest in Washington, D.C.

Other than perhaps the imprint left on the Shroud of Turin, there is no physical description of Jesus. The Gospels reveal nothing. When I was a child, I formulated a mental image of Jesus that has never left me: a grinning, strong-shouldered man; the Good Shepherd with a lamb resting on His shoulders. The Gospel of John brings the metaphor to life: "I am the good shepherd. A good shepherd lays down his life for the sheep." (10:11). This image of Jesus, along with Him stretched out on the cross, was perhaps the dimension of Christ that Dad most wanted me to see—a paternal presence willing to sacrifice, suffer, and die, if necessary, in order to save me. In a sense, Dad probably considered that he wouldn't have been much of a father if he was not willing to sacrifice for his children.

At the 2018 youth synod in Rome, it seems to me that an overeager spirit of listening, openness, and accompaniment was extended to this younger generation of Catholics. In endeavoring to understand their seduction by the modern culture and its underlying disputes with the Church's harder teachings, it seems (at least by my reading of attending bishops' comments and analysis) that bishops at the synod were excessively gracious in "listening," but not very vigorous in lending voice to the majestic truth of the Catholic Church. It would be startling, I imagine, if even one bishop had declared to a single millennial: "Until you make the very real decision to slowly pull away and separate from the culture's flood of false gods, the pouring out of Christ's riches upon your souls simply cannot happen in full." Dad may have lent a "listening" ear to me, but because his wisdom was greater than mine, he had the final say-so, and his convictions were given prominence in our home.

It is as ironic as it is discouraging that bishops had gathered at the youth synod to "listen" to perhaps the most profoundly under-catechized generation of Catholics in Church history. It is also dispiriting and a cruel irony — or at least a rather inconvenient confluence of timing — that these proceedings unfolded in the unseemly shadow of one of the ugliest scandals in Church history, which directly impacts the Church's youth. They are humiliatingly linked. I recall a time when I considered my childhood parish the safest place this side of heaven. *Sigh.* It is a scandal, perhaps, that the synod wasn't canceled altogether as the tattered Church attempts to right herself from her tragically compromised state.

The enormous crisis of fatherhood in the culture is no secret, but less talked about is what a mounting number of Catholics believe to be a crisis of true fatherhood or, put another way, of true masculinity, in the Church. As the lyrical language of monks, saints, mystics, and their priestly forefathers has grown fainter, like the piecemeal extinguishing of Tenebrae candles, a modern strain of what might rightly be called *priestly effeminacy* has swept into parishes. There is no avoiding it. Throughout the land, full-bodied Catholic preaching has become muted, pious customs abandoned, and teachings of the Faith left unarticulated. The breadth of Church teaching, passed on by faithful priests from generation to generation as seamlessly as one neighbor happily shares a cup of sugar with the next, seems in many parishes to have been replaced with fluffier, gentler, and safer messages. The Church's authoritative voice and uninterrupted teachings on the soul-saving efficacy of heroic virtue, a spirit of asceticism, and the quest for holiness seemingly reside now in mostly lonely outposts; an outgrowth of impotency has spread.

In more than a decade, I have not been sharply challenged — in a way men must be challenged — by a priest to grow in holiness (and, oh, do I need to be!). There was a time when I was given a gut check every other Sunday morning. Rarely, though, am I reminded of the rootedness of my sinfulness, the state of my eternal soul, and my need to suffer for holiness.

"Priesthood relates to God, holiness, a desire to be holy as Christ is holy, to be perfect as the heavenly Father is perfect; but also to be a victim for the people — a bearer of the weight of their problems," one priest told me. "But many priests have become very secular, with secular interests. A lot of priests are concerned with planning their day off, their holidays, what they're going to eat that night — whereas always before it was, 'What can I do to build up the faithful and proclaim the Gospel for the people who've drifted?' Priests used to mourn when they saw that their parishioners had drifted."

God the Father is the initiator of human life (with human fathers, who are images of Him); the Church as Bride receives. It stands to reason that when a priest is strong, holy, and intentional, his flock likewise will be. When a priest's care for his flock presents itself as purposeful in his teaching, preaching, and witness, the sheepfold will begin to regard him as a father who gives life. Many thousands of holy saints and priests have offered up their lives to advance the fullness of the Faith. And in dying, they taught the living how to live. They've always taught that the life of virtue involves confronting evil and battling daily with Satan, in order to attain sanctity and heaven.

When priests preach with unmistakable clarity about the Church's moral doctrines and "hard sayings," they'll undoubtedly stun and disturb some in their pews. When they endeavor to teach their own RCIA, Pre-Cana, and catechism classes and generously offer their time for spiritual direction and daily confessions, they might grow weary. When they address the wages of sin, contraception, the reality of hell, and the need for repentance and conversion, a gulf may grow between them and their parishioners, but they will raise a few souls that are seemingly dead. Humiliations will come and go. Bouts of loneliness, abandonment, and misunderstanding may become standard (as it was for Christ), but because of the priest's *fiat*, in time, his flock will begin to regard him as their father. When priests become holy, so will the entire Church.

"If a priest is determined not to lose his soul, as soon as any disorder arises in the parish he must trample underfoot all human considerations as well as the fear of the contempt and hatred of his people," St. John Vianney said. "He must not allow anything to bar his way in the discharge of duty, even where he is certain of being murdered on coming down from the pulpit.

A pastor who wants to do his duty must keep his sword in hand at all times."[31]

The true spiritual father has always stood his ground as an efficacious sign of contradiction to the world, a proclaimer of truth, and a leader of souls to sanctity and heaven. When parishioners regard a priest as their father—the holy shepherd willing to die to help them achieve peace and save their soul—they'll likely meet any demand of his. They'll do so because, in a sense, they understand that his authoritative and paternal voice is simply the instruction of the One he serves.

"In a way, the good priest just reaches out and grabs people," one priest told me, "then shows them the face of Jesus. Then he says, 'Now, go live with Him.'"

[31] Quoted at Saints' Quotes, http://www.saintsquotes.net/Selection%20-%20Priests.html.

11

Availability: The Shepherd's Wellspring of Love

One autumn morning, my brother Danny called me and asked that I drop everything and get to a job site an hour across town. There had been an accident. One of our men lay motionless on the ground.

When I arrived, what seemed like miles of yellow caution tape stretched into every corner of a broad cul-de-sac, choking me off from our company's stunned bricklayers and mason tenders, who were sitting in a quiet line on the curb. For the first time, they seemed gentle. Their coworker, a stocky, good-natured young man in his early twenties, was dead. A piece of construction equipment had fallen on him. I always called him Goose, a character in a movie he had loved.

I knocked on his El Salvadoran parents' door an hour later to tell them that their son had lost his life. His mother fell to the worn carpet her son had walked on just hours earlier. She screamed as if she had been tomahawked. Her husband went stone-faced. The deceased's sister translated through her sobs. "They want to see him," she said. "Drive us to him."

At the hospital, their torment increased. Administrators wouldn't permit entrance to his room until after the body was examined. Trapped by my inability to speak in their native tongue, my words of attempted tenderness arrived as inelegant, ruinous gestures. I sweated. And after some time, I just stood empty near them, chin-high in the drowning waves of what seemed like a nightmare.

Somehow, as if an angel had placed it there, a thought came. I remembered hearing of a Spanish-speaking priest at the parish down the road. I can't account for where this thought came from, outside of God's kindness and whispered providence.

The moon was just rising when I called the church office from a still-existing pay phone. I had no cell. "Good evening. This is Our Lady of Lourdes. How can I help you?" asked a kind voice.

"Is there a priest there who speaks Spanish? There's an emergency."

"Do you mean Fr. Dorsonville?"

"If he speaks Spanish."

"I believe he's here. Let me check."

The crackle of the phone offered a song of hope. After several minutes, a man answered with a lyrical, lively accent. As I unloaded the story in stumbling fashion, he listened noiselessly.

"Wait by the entrance. In ten minutes, I'll be there."

I saw his collar first. Then I noticed the Irish derby covering his shiny head and a long black jacket. He strode toward me, his merry eyes penetrating mine, and this mysterious priest was *smiling*. He grabbed my left forearm and stood directly in front of me. The tip of his nose was a mere foot from mine. He looked deep into my red-rimmed eyes. "Go home now," he commanded gently but firmly. "I will handle things from here. Your family needs you. And you need your family."

I thought, "But he doesn't even know who the family is. He doesn't know their location." I told him I'd lead him to them.

"Kevin," he said, smiling. "Go home to your wife."

He turned away from me. The automatic doors slid open as he moved inside and reached to remove his derby, so he could present himself as a gentleman and a mannerly priest.

For the entirety of the next week, Fr. Dorsonville plunged into this family's valley of anguish. And he just stayed there. He warmed their hollowed-out souls with his sunny personality, benevolence, and intentional availability for them. The mourners kept dragging themselves back to this mysterious priest because he provided what seemed their only pinhole of light. As the week progressed, I became his part-time personal chauffeur as I escorted him into different homes of the grieving, to meeting places of the deceased's loved ones, where I marveled as he spoke foreign words that reached their souls. He untangled confusion, decompressed vengeance, and redirected fury aimed at God, gently demythologizing Him as a heartless, absentee Father. With a humility borne of wisdom, he delicately escorted this impoverished family into the mystery of God and opened Catholic thought on the strange ways of His providence. I remembered continually thinking that, a week before this, he hadn't even known that this family, or I, even existed. Each of us was drained; he was filled with adrenaline.

Fr. Dorsonville never left Goose's family. At the gravesite, dozens of weeping family members remained until the operator of the cemetery Bobcat scooped the last of the soil into the opening in the earth. The gravediggers completed their work and departed beneath darkening skies. But the mourners, whose sorrow had grown to a crescendo pitch, chose to stay. Many wailed inconsolably. So Fr. Dorsonville stayed with them, head bowed, an inaudible witness to their grief. His kindness was now forever stamped on this family's souls. He had become one of them.

Today, all these years later, this family and many of their friends recognize Fr. Dorsonville as another Christ.

The Priests We Need to Save the Church

This is what a priest does. He makes himself available, enters into disconsolation and all the dark and tragic parts of people's lives, stays there, and saves. And when he does, he often changes everything.

I discovered later that Fr. Dorsonville—now a bishop in Washington, D.C.—was once a close friend of Tommy.

"Tommy was one who helped show me what a priest does," Bishop Mario Dorsonville said. "This is who a priest is. Tommy was a priest always filled with great joy because he spent his entire priesthood serving others. People loved him because he served them."

Case in point: Fire codes were broken at my uncle's funeral. Roads were shut down and traffic redirected. Some news reports estimated that more than three thousand mourners had poured into Sacred Heart Church, where Tommy began his ministry. It wasn't just the laity who loved him; priests from three or four dioceses attended his funeral. It took ten minutes for the 250 priests, deacons, and seminarians to process in at the beginning of the Mass. This included seven young men whom Tommy had recently led to the seminary. "The Wells guys" they call them, even to this day.

It has become clear to me what attracted those waves of mourners to his funeral: Tommy's spirited vigilance for his flock. In the aftermath of his murder, one of the detectives found Tommy's Day-Timer in the rectory and started flipping pages to hunt for clues in it. He later mentioned to the press that he had never come across a calendar with more penned-in commitments. Second to his devotion to the Eucharist, his availability for people became perhaps the most identifiable mark of his priestly mission. He was subservient to it; everything else—be it sleep, privacy, downtime, fatigue—took a backseat to his attempts to build God's kingdom.

From the moment his alarm sounded in the morning to the time he fell into bed at night, he welcomed individuals into his life as a shepherd of their souls. Unless he was in prayer, it was difficult to find him alone, but it was from his devotion to the inner life of prayer and the immensity of his faith in God that his availability sprang.

"I can't think of a single time in my life when he wasn't there for me," said former parishioner Rich Mulhare. "Whether he had to set me straight on something I was doing wrong, marking an important event in my life, or leading me to make a life-changing decision, he made a point to show up. Since his death, I've searched everywhere for a moral compass with the presence and mind of Fr. Wells. There isn't one."

Tommy realized that simplistic solutions don't exist in regard to matters of the soul, so he spent what may have seemed an inordinate amount of time with parishioners until an illuminated path emerged. "Somehow he seemed to find a way to make himself available for everyone — and everyone wanted him," friend and former parishioner Tommy Sheehan said. "Weddings, Baptisms, spiritual direction, to have dinner with [him] — Fr. Wells was a priest in extremely high demand, but I remember him telling me that this was what a priest did. We were driving to a wedding way out in the middle of nowhere, and he turned to me and said, 'This is why a priest can never be married. He's got to be around whenever someone needs him.'"

Perhaps it was just providence, but at the start of his ministry, Tommy was blessed to live in a parish rectory in the heart of a middle-class neighborhood filled with young families. It was a time when flannel-shirted teenage boys wore their hair shaggy and long, and girls had a heightened sense of liberation in the wake of the changes brought about by the cultural movements of the 1960s. Social tensions were beginning to fray the nerves of moms and dads and cause dissension in homes and at his Sacred Heart parish.

As countercultural behaviors in the new hippie movement became realities to contend with, parents sensed that they could share their concerns with the neighborly, young new priest in town. They'd see him washing his car in front of the rectory in cut-off jeans and a collar, exchanging pleasantries with whoever strolled by. As angst-ridden parents gravitated to him to share their concerns, Tommy often threw his head back in gently mocking laughter and begged them not to worry. If they persisted, he'd often howl: "Where's your trust in God?!" Then he'd sigh, shake his head, and mock some more—*tsk, tsk, tsk, tsk*—a mild display of disappointment. This simple gesture became his trademark, and he always returned to it because of its uncanniness at cutting the tension and redirecting souls to pure, absolute trust in God. That question about trust went on to become the soundtrack of his priestly life; he asked it of hundreds of parishioners down the years.

After calming moms' and dads' nerves, he promised to engage with their teenagers—as long as they promised to have full trust in God's providence.

Thereafter, most evenings he'd walk the streets with his jet-black mutt, Parcheese, and introduce himself to his new neighbors—the Muldoons, the Bournes, the McIntyres, the Kellys, the Ambrosinis, the Browns, the Kellys, the Fitzmaurices, the Wiebers, and others—and shoot the breeze with them. After some time, teenagers began to filter out of their homes to meet in the middle of the street with the long-sideburned, gregarious priest; it became a custom in the "Buckingham" section of Bowie.

Teens learned that he wasn't a collar-wearing defiance to their newborn '70s autonomy; they saw that he just wanted to help shape it. He spoke from what seemed a sunniness of the heart. Nothing he said, they noticed, was half-hearted or had a ring of false companionship; he spoke their language. He saw the teens as deserving of his respect and care, so he didn't judge their hairstyles, bell-bottomed jeans, irreverence, or even the cigarette- or pot-smoking hippie they may have been dating at the time. Once the teens were within his orbit, though, each of those issues would be addressed.

He brought the celebratory language of heaven and Christ's intense love into conversations, homilies, and spiritual direction. He knew that, once young Catholics experienced God's transcendence, understood His distinct plan for their lives, and became sanctified in His truth and in the Church's doctrines, they would desire to travel any road to encounter God even more deeply. This was his plan of action:

1. Encounter an individual with a startling buoyancy.
2. Devote energy and time to building a relationship.
3. Introduce and clarify the realities of the Catholic Faith.
4. Create a soul bound for heaven.

Tommy gave himself away in this manner to the hundreds, perhaps thousands, of souls, who were willing to walk alongside him for the next twenty-nine years.

"It really did happen this way. You'd see Fr. Wells come walking up the street in the evenings with that dog. And the first thing you saw was that smile. Joy was pouring out of him. He just had it," said Mike Ambrosini, a long-haired, rambunctious teenager in those days. "And everyone would start pouring out of their houses after dinner to speak with him.

"A lot of friendships began with us back then, but we began to realize that he was going to hold each of us to account," Mike said. "If he was going to go all in with us, we needed to go all in with him. And we stayed with him because we knew he was real and sensed that what he was telling us about the Faith was true. My friends and I began seeing that he was a priest who wanted to enter into your life, to really get to know you—but there was no mistaking the relationship; he was going to make it a point to bring the Catholic Faith and God's love into it."

Mike's friendship with Tommy early in his priesthood became a lifelong friendship. "Throughout my life, when I needed to see him about a problem, he made sure he was there. But he had this way with me: he would always turn the thing around and start banging on me to become better for my wife and for my family. I told him about a problem I was having with my wife, and he gave me a fair shake, but then he said, 'I understand the issue, Mike, but guess what—I want you to carry her baggage now. You're a man, right? You hold the bag now.' He put the whole thing back on me, and he changed our marriage because of it. He wanted me to suffer for her because—and I mean this—he wanted me to become a saint."

Tommy knew that if teenagers (or anyone, for that matter) had the Faith explained in its fullness, with intentionality and a radiant joy, their hearts would be leavened, drawn in, and eventually the teenagers would desire to embark on a life committed to the Church's teachings. It would have been easy for dissenting parishioners at Sacred Heart to slap down the young priest's zealous company-line orthodox approach during that rebellious time in America, but they saw that he had a gift for stitching eternal truths into a cohesive whole for a widely diverse group of people. He'd touch the pro-contraception feminist in one place, the daily communicant in another; he'd direct the zealot's wildfire here and urge the Jimi Hendrix fan there. His sermons during those days often held his Irish-tough pastor, Msgr. John Hogan, spellbound. Hogan said that his young charge was the only priest he had ever known who was able to gain consensus with Catholics on opposite sides of the political spectrum. "We had difficult days in the beginning between the conservatives and liberals, but he could bring them all together," Msgr. Hogan, now deceased, told the *Washington Post*. "He was really an exceptional priest in every way."[32]

Until the day of his murder, Tommy honored his promise to the once-angst-ridden Bowie parents: he maintained close friendships with many of those dozens of teenagers over the span of thirty years. The majority of those hippies wound up marrying Catholics and raising their families in the Faith. Today, some share with their grandchildren stories of their uncommon priest friend, Tommy.

My uncle's patron saints were St. Thomas More and St. John Vianney. Like More, Tommy was unbending in the uncompromising truths of the Faith. But it was his bond with Vianney that most visibly shaped his priesthood. Arguably, the greatest proof of love for Jesus Christ and His Church is the laying down of one's own physical life, because the martyr's blood always becomes a signpost to those left in his or her wake. Like Vianney, though, Tommy accepted a different form of martyrdom: the daily, unremitting grind of being wholly available for those in need of a priestly presence.

After studying Vianney and speaking with innumerable folks who've been influenced by Tommy, I think that the slow-motion

---

[32] Hamil R. Harris "An Exceptional Priest" *Washington Post*, June 22, 2000, https://www.washingtonpost.com/archive/local/2000/06/22/an-exceptional-priest/ba3dd6c9-20ae-4876-b0f5-d6a4526ad554/?utm_term=.85c7218e843b.

martyrdom of round-the-clock availability holds an even higher degree of heroism than the laying down of one's life at a particular moment. An arrow penetrating the heart is neat and swift; Vianney's thousands of cumulative hours of hearing daily confessions and 2:00 a.m. risings to start each day, I believe, are of even higher form. And Tommy's countless and continual dives into thousands of souls down the years could, I believe, be regarded in the same light.

The paradoxical, brutal fruit of real romance — Vianney and Tommy knew this interior reality as intimately as anyone — is the daily and simple deaths for one's beloved. Their priestly vocation to edify, transform, and save souls meant doing battle with evil and sin. But it also meant *showing up* again and again. Folks flooded to Ars because they sensed there was a father abiding there, one who would suffer relentlessly for them. In a way, it was the same for Tommy, who understood man's deep need for God — and the meaninglessness of a life without Him. His persistent willingness to help mend broken souls made him like the shepherd Christ spoke of in the Gospel of John:

> A good shepherd lays down his life for his sheep. A hired man who is not a shepherd and whose sheep are not his own, sees a wolf coming and leaves the sheep and runs away, and the wolf catches and scatters them. This is because he works for pay and has no concern for the sheep. I am the good shepherd, and I know mine and mine know me, just as the Father knows me and I know the Father; and I will lay down my life for the sheep. (John 10:11–15)

Tommy understood that God had blessed him with a rollickingly cheerful nature, so he strove to radiate it to help warm the anguished. Because he had a sixth sense for identifying others' pain, the hours of his days became long and laborious. He was seldom in his rectory. He simply wanted to transmit the radiance within him to others, whether to a small child, a lapsed Catholic, an agnostic, a champion sinner, or the guy pumping gas next to him. Sts. Philip Neri, John Bosco, and Francis de Sales passed along a similar type of sacred joy.

Greg Emerson met Tommy as a troubled fifth-grade student. "It was a tough school, and I lived in the principal's office. It seemed like I was getting into fist fights every day," Greg said of his tumultuous childhood. "Mom was tired of it. She knew things were getting dangerous in my life and that there needed to be a change. She pulled me out at the end of the school year and found the nearest church with a school. We didn't have a lot of money for a private education, but something had to give. Then she found St. Mark's and met Fr. Wells."

Greg wasn't raised Catholic; his Mom had left the Faith. But Tommy struck a deal with her: if Greg agreed to visit him at St. Mark's rectory each week for a personalized RCIA class, he would be admitted into the Catholic school, and at a reduced rate.

"I always thought Catholic schools were for a bunch of sissies," Greg said. "Then—I'll never forget—I met this priest who changed everything. And it happened in an instant. I was hopping on my bike and racing out to him when my Mom couldn't drive me out. Fr. Wells started with the Ten Commandments, and in no time, I became immersed in everything he was throwing at me. By the end of the summer, he had changed me. I'd say all these years later that he saved my life—and could have saved my soul.

"But the thing that got me was that this priest never blew me off. You could see he was very busy and in demand, but I just kept riding my bike to that rectory, and he'd always be in there waiting for me for my class. I could see it in every fiber of his being and in those smiling, bright blue eyes: he loved Jesus Christ and being a priest. That joy became contagious to me. It was the best summer of my life because I saw that he had made himself available just for me."

My uncle was just one more in a long line of determined, grind-it-out priests who understood that their flock was caught up in a war until the end of time. Satan wants those souls under his care. So does God. And Tommy knew a bachelorhood-style of priesthood wasn't going to cut it.

Vianney walked around his village with a catechism tucked beneath his arm and taught the Faith to the children under his care. Tommy devoted an enormous amount of time teaching CCD, RCIA, Pre-Cana, and catechism classes. He could have passed off the lion's share of this work to catechists, but he didn't. He became legendary in classrooms for his exuberance, humor, and animated teaching method, which included deep measures of theology, absorbing storytelling, practical advice, and hilarity. He knew that a captive audience was a prime opportunity for God to work through him, so he took full advantage of it. A troubled teenager named Gina Pecher was in one of those classrooms at St. Mark's in Adelphi, Maryland. After being captivated by Tommy's warmth and love for Christ, she shared with him her turmoil over her a contentious relationship with her nonbelieving mother. She sensed in Tommy someone who'd tend to her pain.

"When he saw that I was broken, he told me to contact him any time of the day or night," Gina said. "So over and over, I just cried to him, but he just stayed jovial, focused on the positive, offered Christ-centered wisdom, and prayed with me. He always trusted that God would work it out.

"He became my Father," Gina added. "He took me on as his frightened, little daughter in darkness, and he pulled me out. I will love him forever for it. God knew how wounded I was, and I think He pitied me. His answer was sending me Msgr. Wells.

"There was no one like him and there never will be. He made the time for me, just another a troubled teenager. To this day, he guides my life. He was the shepherd who fed me, who was there for me."

12

The Prophetic Voice in the Desert

A few hundred high schoolers and college students surged into the Catholic church to mourn their wildly popular, cheery-faced friend Gaby, who had lost her prolonged fight to control throbbing blood vessels in her brain. In the midst of her struggle, she'd embraced an achingly beautiful conversion to the Catholic Faith, bringing her dad to conversion in the process.

From the outset of the funeral Mass, teenagers texted, openly conversed, whispered, and even flirted. The majority of young mourners seemed to be nonpracticing Catholics, alien to the Faith, or perhaps had never before attended a Mass. They were charmingly irreverent within an unfamiliar landscape of rubrics and sacred rites—and each of the faithful funeral-going Catholics had the sense to extend charity in their allowance of it.

The sustained buzz from the pews was nothing new to the pastor. Virtually all priests have celebrated dozens of similar Masses, most likely at weddings and funerals.

But this priest wasn't like most priests—Tommy had motivated him early on in his priesthood to commit to the occasionally incommodious work of saving souls.

Processing to the altar at the start of Mass, he saw that he was passing what seemed a vast meadow of roaming sheep. The cell phone–laden pews were overfull with distracted activity. As had become his custom in such situations, he saw an opening impregnated with the possibility of conversion. Instinctually, he desired to carry each soul onto a lusher landscape, one bursting with truth, sustenance, and heightened consciousness. So the Spirit led this priest to escort the uncatechized mourners into the mind of their friend on the final trip he had taken to see her.

Following the Gospel, he took a few moments to take in the gathering before him, as you might imagine Jesus looking with tenderness upon the hungry faces spread out before Him on a sun-swept hillside. Then he opened his mouth and took them by the hand, slowly and deliberately leading them into the story of the young heroine who lay in the casket before them.

He described the gloom of Gaby's hospital room during his last visit, and introduced the long needle, spreading his hands to demonstrate its considerable length. The needle was thicker than normal, he explained, because it was made to penetrate deep into skulls. The texting and giggles slowed. He said a doctor would plunge the needle thirty times into her cranium and her brain. These excruciating injections of botox, he explained, were necessary to cushion the unwieldy malformation and prevent the rupture that would instantly kill her. Gaby hadn't wanted anyone to know about this painful treatment, though. The church fell silent.

Minutes before her doctor applied the first shot, this teenage girl suddenly spoke of her friends, spilling all that was in her heart. She told the priest that she worried about the ones caught up in serious sin. She said she was concerned for their souls. The priest thumbed blessed oil onto her forehead as she continued. Her newfound faith had helped her surrender her terror of death, her debilitating headaches, and her bodily pain as an act of sacrificial love. But she told him she wished to go deeper. She wanted to offer her crown of thorns for the conversion of her closest friends.

So, with the first excruciating injection, she called out a friend's name, then another. Thirty first names were set free, like puffs of incense rising to the open hands of her Savior. "Here Lord, take her. Bring her to awareness of You."

No one moved in the pews.

Within two minutes, the strange purposing of mortification, and the eloquent manner in which a friend cuts a path to sainthood merged. The heroism of this young dead girl had been displayed in its full glory, and awareness of the meaning of sacrificial love cascaded into the pews. The weight of the priest's words within his masterful storytelling was disorienting, so many just wept and dropped their heads onto the shoulders of the persons beside them. Others looked saucer-eyed, seemingly pulled into a place of full-on wonder. The priest's story seemed to ignite flames of sudden introspection into their consciences, where the weight of sinfulness was perhaps considered for the first time. "Had she called my name? Was I one?"

It seemed a slow-motion, church-wide transfiguration, so no one dared even whisper, lest they say something foolish. Lives changed that day because a priest made a decision to bend his message to address the mostly uncatechized assembly before him. He knew their tears of sorrow would signify little. Their eulogies would be forgotten. All that mattered to this priest was that the young mourners were taken by the hand to the deeper reality that abided undiscovered within them.

At the beginning of Mass, the priest understood that he had to slash through thickets of distraction and carelessness to penetrate souls. His response was the story of Gaby, the young heroine who had intentionally decided to live out her Catholic Faith in the most agonizing moments of her life. *She*—not he—would lead them to the deeper reality of faith. I wouldn't dare to presume that the majority of mourners raced out to find the nearest RCIA sign-up sheet, but I imagine very few young mourners left the church that day unchanged by the manner in which the priest's words and preaching opened up a different dimension to their friend's life.

"When he preaches, a priest must make the call to conversion. It seems a lot of priests have forgotten this—every homily should have at its heart an attempt to draw people to holiness," the priest said. "[At the funeral,] if I tried to meet the young mourners with something topical or relevant to their lives—say I brought up [the television shows] *Two and a Half Men* or *Survivor* or whatever they might be watching—I'm absolutely betraying who I am as a priest. My purpose as a priest is to bring others to conversion. If they see my call as real and that I'm fighting for them and their soul, then they know it's done out of love, and very often there will be a response.

"It's like the dad who speaks to his trouble teenage son from the heart. He's able to penetrate because the son realizes Dad's words come from a place of deep love for him. This dad, and the priest, simply have to penetrate the heart. Because it's in the heart where conversion begins."

Within the feverish pace of our technological, text-heavy, word-thin universe, it is the prophetic voice of the holy Catholic priest that seems best able to spark conversion in individuals, families, neighborhoods, and entire communities. Regardless of where a true priest finds himself in these storm-plagued days of the Church, he carries with him the muscled, time-tested words of salvation, and his words have the power to set fires of enlightenment in darkened souls.

"Everything spoken by a priest should be of Christ," said Fr. Martin Flum of St. Michael's parish in rural Maryland. "Carrying the prophetic office is difficult, but if the voice goes silent—if people sense that the voice of the priest isn't convicted or drawn from Christ Himself—there will be trouble."

Although my parents taught each of their children that the centerpiece of the Mass was the Eucharist, I often found myself hanging on each syllable preached by my parish priests and those from the neighboring parish. The convicting and soul-catching words of Fr. Goode, Irish-brogued Fr. Cassin, or even Msgr. Hogan from the parish across town consistently managed to stretch my imagination and take me to the wild land of my untamed curiosity. These were apostolic men who cared for souls. They were most effective at the weekday school Mass, when their revelatory words bore into me like the Ghost of Christmas Past. *Maybe that lie to Mom about taking the two quarters on her dresser was rotten after all.* Their homilies were disruptions that pricked my conscience—nudging reminders of the consequences of small sins, the perils of cruelty to my classmates, and the repercussions of an unchecked will. So that I wouldn't be lulled into complacent acceptance of (for example) my round-the-clock teasing of my sisters, these preachers pried open my eyes to *see* Jesus at Golgotha—the blood-caked creases of His loincloth, the barbed crown of three-inch-long thorns, His deep-purple knee gashes, His utter aloneness, with low canopies of dark clouds skimming the blackening sky. Streaks of dark blood oozed down the cross as thick-legged Roman soldiers mocked Jesus, but these homilies made me see that my own sinfulness mocked—*and teased*—Him as well. With them, I yelled, "Crucify him!" My sinfulness had played a part. Mary was grief-stricken at the foot of the cross, but her tears ran because of her pure love for Jesus, not just because of the horror unfolding before her. I, too, played a part in her sorrow. Jesus shivered virtually companionless on the cross, but these priests offered a wider lens: I, too, left Him stranded when I chose to neglect prayer and abandon the warmth of His friendship.

Now that you see the state of your soul, Kevin, let's talk about consoling Him.

Today, such a preaching style might result in a priest's being thrown into solitary confinement. But I wouldn't have wanted it any differently, because happily, as quickly as they had led me into the consequential valley of my unruliness and sin, those manly priests threw me on their backs and carried me to theological mountaintops, where only saints roamed. Stories of warriors who had traded suffering for glory flooded my soul with flowering desire. "Why couldn't I live on an island, loving forgotten lepers, like Damien of Molokai?" "God wants you to" would be a conventional response. "But the habit of virtue is hard. Damien achieved it. Fight for it. And you can be as strong as he was."

These priests revealed saints as *men*; in their preaching, they were spiritual fathers to my soul. The bracing intentionality behind their words took me to the post-Pentecost Upper Room and set me face-to-face with a roomful of soon-to-be martyrs, who turned their chairs toward me, squared their shoulders, and spoke to me about the elegant, brutal secrets of bravery. I chose St. Paul for my confirmation saint because Fr. Cassin — who became aware of my desire to write — painted for me an icon of this sword-carrying, letter-writing immovable apostle who brought more people to Christ than any man in the history of the world. And it was Fr. Cassin who revealed to me what a modern-day St. Paul looked like as he walked door to door on summer evenings to visit each Levitt-built house of my Bowie hometown, extending invitations for thousands of strangers to become parishioners at his St. Pius X parish. That witness was box-office gold to my soul, which strived for more.

As I grew older, however, and began to understand the Mass more fully as the true-to-form memorialization of the Last Supper and of Christ's sacrificial death on Calvary, the homily lost some of its impact. I considered a well-delivered sermon an added Mass bonus—and a poorly prepared, meandering one something to be (most of the time) charitably endured. But it was throughout my dark hospital stay—when a chorus of mocking demons had taken up real estate in my neuro-ICU room—that the transformative power of priests' words broke into me like rescuing companies of guardian angels. On the most gnawing of those days, when I repeatedly and hallucinogenically *saw* my seven-year-old daughter Gabby drowning in the ceiling tiles above while being mocked by demons for my inability to save her, I knew I needed assistance. A series of procedures had failed to embolize my coursing blood, death seemed guaranteed, and I began to consider my soul's fate. As my prognosis worsened, Krista began to ask people to pray for my soul, nothing more. Thereafter, beneath cold January skies, a band of determined priests began traveling to my hospital in Baltimore to whisper homilies into my ear.

One by one, they'd assume a post at my bedside, like lantern holders in Gethsemane, and work to heal me. Although my wrists were secured to the bedrails and tubes, shunts, and wires were fastened to virtually every uncovered part of my face and skull, I was *free* when they crouched down to shine clarifying words of hope into the caverns of my soul. Their words chased away the terror of demons and doubts and created space for consolation to pass into me. As I was on the edge of death, these priests, like the men who called to Bartimaeus, "Take courage; get up, Jesus is calling you" (see Mark 10:49), made me believe I could be well.

This saving team of priests couldn't have been aware of it (because my power of speech had been rendered mostly useless), but their theologically textured teaching on total surrender to God's way eventually drove me to consent to it tranquilly: convincing me was difficult for them; obliging was difficult for me. While my eyes were sealed shut to the world, those priests painted landscapes of knightly heroism, speaking of the well-carried cross, of blind surrender to divine providence, and, with burning conviction, of my need to conform to Christ—and nothing else. Their words of trustful surrender seemed to come from the lips of a resurrected Lazarus and even from Jesus Himself, who was now helping to shoulder *my own cross* alongside me.

"Jesus can heal you," those priests said. "Don't doubt Him."

All these years later, after hearing many whispered hospital homilies on hope, doubt has crept in—not into my own faith or my belief in the potency of God, but into many of the priests who preach on Christ's divinity and His majestic Church. As a former sportswriter who was transferred repeatedly to bureaus throughout Florida, I became a new parishioner (if memory serves) at eight Catholic churches over a course of a few years. In the process, I learned quickly that scrutinizing the homilies of my parish priest was not only unprofitable but did little more than disturb my soul and spiral it downward. During this time, I noticed clearly what seemed a conspiracy of silence, or a suppression of many of the concrete Catholic realities I had received as a child. Soul-stirring homilies pieced together from the bottomless treasure house of the Faith were exchanged for "insights" or socially conscious dialogues contoured to fit what was culturally permissible. The long and noble march toward sanctity, the pursuit of virtue, hell, sin, supernatural grace, and the rest barely got whispers; they were replaced by careful watchwords. Rather than being encouraged to climb for the martyr's crown, it seemed as if the flock was invited simply to rest their fleshy arms and elbows on the ladder's third or fourth rung.

It was often at Mass, in fact, that I felt caught up in a Matrix-like alternate universe, where homilies addressed anything and everything, except for what really mattered for eternity. The storm-whipped seas just outside the parish's hurricane-proof doors hardly got a nod. Pew sitters never squirmed because the priest never squirmed within his preaching bubble. A mystifying and fragmentary retreat from the religion of Christ had begun, or at least a flight from many magisterial truths, and I noticed its diminishment week in and week out. My blood, though, never boiled. Often, instead, a line I'd read from C. S. Lewis' *The Screwtape Letters* came to mind then, as it has frequently since: "A moderated religion is as good for us [demons] as no religion at all—and more amusing."[33]

"Strong homilies have diminished as societal standards have diminished," Fr. Larry Swink said. "It's sad, but a lot of priests have decided to no longer confront sin. Many seem to have sipped the Kool-Aid of cultural political correctness, and that's a serious problem. A priest is a father first, and as a father, he must address his spiritual children, and sometimes correct them."

A lost library of muscular teaching on the ordered Catholic life and toeing the moral line seems to be found today only in old, small-print Catholic books. Preaching used to be rather

---

[33] C. S. Lewis, *The Screwtape Letters* (New York: HarperOne, 2009), 170.

straightforward: priests exposed the way of righteousness, "to be holy and without blemish before him" (Eph. 1:4), and the way of sin. The first brought your soul into eternity; the second didn't.

Due to the sacramental character given to them at Ordination, priests are inescapably bound to preach with the clear and prophetic voice of Christ. Instead, many priests seem emasculated, having chosen to plant their flag within a contaminated landscape of safe preaching, where sin, moral landslides, redefinitions of natural law, and cultural flotsam — which priests once felt duty-bound to confront, dissect, and work to annihilate — are left to fester and spread. It could be easily argued that because our Church has absorbed much of the secular values of the world, her priests have adopted a less rigorous or more socially conscious style of preaching. Homilies that focus on God's mercy (without explaining to the flock that the fullest measure of God's mercy is found in absolution in the confessional), bringing "Christ's face into the world" (without elucidating Jesus' thornier *spiritual* works of mercy), and accompaniment (without defining its contours and limits) are normative, and even the trend, in many American churches.

"Many priests have made the decision to contracept God's truth and Church teaching. They've contracepted their mouths," one priest told me. "Their preaching is marked by absence rather than life."

Weak homilies that leave faint imprints on souls have plagued the Church before, so advice from the saints is much needed. Pope St. Gregory the Great said in the sixth century: "Pastors who lack foresight hesitate to say openly what is right because they fear losing the favor of men," he wrote. "As the voice of truth tells us, such leaders are not zealous pastors who protect their flocks; rather, they are like mercenaries who flee by taking refuge in silence when the wolf appears. The Lord reproaches them through the prophet: 'They are dumb dogs that cannot bark.'[34]

Msgr. Rossetti, who has contended with Satan as the Washington, D.C., Archdiocesan exorcist for more than ten years, said that it's a mistake for priests to go completely silent on the reality of hell. Recently, he has been in contact with a religious mystic who, according to Msgr. Rossetti, had a spiritual vision of hell. An angel had led him to a mountain overlooking a sweeping expanse of hell, where he took in graphic displays of grotesquely lewd and malevolent violence inflicted upon "millions" of damned souls. In one scene: teams of demons pressed their claws and misshapen fingers into the damned, who were lined up awaiting entrance into hell. The screams of the tortured were "ear piercing" as their pleas for mercy were ignored.

The images "made a searing and lasting impression on me," Msgr. Rossetti said. "But they fall right in line with what the mystics of the past saw in hell. Hell is real. This is not something we made up. Jesus clearly speaks of 'a weeping and gnashing of teeth.' A priest doesn't need to mention the reality of hell every week, but hell can be a pretty good motivator. The stakes are high. Souls are on the line."

Given that mortal sin and hell seem to be so rarely discussed from the pulpit, there does seem to be a widespread cadre of priests that have accepted a contemporary view of hell that seems to be gaining steam today: that hell exists, but it is empty. But the reality, uncomfortable though it may be, is that Jesus Christ discussed hell often, more than any figure in Scripture. The Son of God said it was a place "where the worm does not die, and

---

[34] Quoted at The Defender, http://www.thedefender.org/POPE%20 SAINT%20GREGORY%20THE%20GREAT.html.

the fire is not quenched" (Mark 9:48). Preaching "around" a just God who punishes egregious sin is a rejection of Christ's direct manner of preaching.

Sound preaching is tantamount to illuminating souls, so I've often wondered, in the aftermath of Tommy's murder and my near-death experience, whether its impoverishment has been the greatest cause for the exodus of once-practicing Catholics, and the deformation of many who have stayed. Ideally, a priest's homily should form the mind, shape the soul, and captivate the heart. But a long line of research polls continually reveal that Catholics around the globe are estranged from the Church. They've walked away from the Faith for a myriad of reasons: clergy sin, insipid liturgies, the eroding of instruction in the Faith, lack of transparency in the hierarchy, a de-emphasis of the sacramental life, and so forth. But also, a sensualized culture that subconsciously hungers for lasting spiritual food is perhaps being left unfed by preaching far different from that of John the Baptist, who preached on conversion, heroic living, and preparation for Christ's coming. In this age dominated by relativism, the lines between good and evil and truth and falsehood are often left open to one's own interpretation in ambiguous homilies that often seem to straddle rather than to pierce.

Priests are ordained to become signs of contradiction in the world, but some seminarians and priests have told me that seminary formators taught them to preach to the "middle" (somewhere between the orthodox and the liberal minded). Scripture clearly indicates, though, that Jesus never preached to percentages or sensibilities. He spoke plainly, as His Father desired. I've also often heard it said that priests' homilies should last seven to ten minutes, but I doubt Jesus considered the amount of time it might take to lead even a single soul to His Father. Because we've each been blackened by the Fall, we're hardly paragons of humility, fidelity to virtue, and charity. As sons and daughters of Adam and Eve, each of us needs to be consistently steered away from sin and to our homeland as sheep must be led to safe pasture. Timid preaching, aimed at the "middle" or restricted within time frames, seems likes an egregious abandonment of a flock, a grievous omission—an opening that would allow devouring wolves to enter.

For the first time in the history of civilization, the traditional family lies victim to the rampant undertow of materialism, relativism, and debauched behaviors. Disordered sexual inclinations and gender fluidity are hailed as good, as abortions, habitual pornography viewing, shacking up, and no-fault divorce have flourished in society. And costuming oneself in ignorance in the face of this anti-person onslaught that surrounds families is perhaps as deadly a form of priestly spiritual sloth as the Church has ever experienced. At its best, priests' silence on this apocalyptic complex of sins reveals a crisis of cowardice; at its worst, their willful neglect reflects something ominous.

"Today, a priest who doesn't have courage isn't a shepherd; he would seem to be just a hireling," one priest told me. "If the priest isn't willing to go to the mat for his flock to share the fullness of the truth of the gospel, he simply isn't a shepherd. He's left his flock wide open and unguarded in the pasture—ripe for being devoured."

Preaching seems to tell the story of a priest's entire ministry. Since my recovery, as I've become more attuned to homilies at Mass, I've seen that a priest's identity is most laid bare when he preaches. For example, if he occasionally mentions a thought that came to him in front of the Blessed Sacrament, or if he draws on a story from St. Teresa of Avila or St. John of the Cross, or perhaps of how he's interrupted by the same barking Saint Bernard during his neighborhood Rosary walks, then his parishioners can safely assume that he's a priest devoted to prayer and steeped in Catholic thought. Conversely, if a priest infrequently mentions the Eucharist, the graces obtained at Adoration, or the necessity of being in a state of grace prior to receiving Communion, he probably doesn't place value in the Eucharist. As a priest ordained to become Christ, he has agreed to consecrate everything to Him; his identity, mission, message, and even his life must be surrendered in shepherding his flock more deeply into the gospel. So, if his preaching lacks vigor or rings hollow, sounds timid or insincere, he would seem to mark himself as disobedient to his identity. In the book of Revelation, John records God's stern words for those uncommitted to a life of faith. "I know about your activities: how you are neither cold nor hot. I wish you were one or the other, but since you are neither hot nor cold, but only lukewarm, I will spit you out of my mouth" (Rev. 3:15–16).

In the course of speaking with many dozens of Tommy's former parishioners for this book, two qualities of his consistently emerged. They recall his building his ministry on his devotion to the Eucharist, and they remember his charism for reaching the depth of souls through his penetrating preaching. They said his homilies were animated by a pressing conviction to lead people away from sin, into virtue, and eventually to heaven. His joy-filled words, former parishioners said, seemed to have sprung from his having *met* Jesus in the Eucharist; and because he *knew* the Author of "his" words, he was better able to hook parishioners. Interestingly, when priests recall Tommy's ministry, many say that the startling power of his preaching was built entirely on the foundation of the Eucharist. If the Eucharist was his sun, his words were its rays; and as the sun increases in brightness on its climb into the sky, the power of his words also swelled to reach more deeply into hearts.

"Each of Fr. Wells's homilies, I believe, came to him in front of the Blessed Sacrament. That's where they took root," Fr. Shaffer said. "He knew Jesus in the Eucharist, and I think that's why so many people ended up loving him as a homilist. That's where he drew his power. His preaching—its depth, humor, storytelling, teaching, the way he connected things, the no-nonsense stuff—it came off so powerfully because he cared for his parishioners' souls, and that love came from his love of the Eucharist."

Often, in the midst of preaching, when Tommy was on the verge of uncovering a vital or potentially polemic teaching, he would fall silent and sway back and forth on the balls of his feet. He'd tilt his head skyward as if looking through an unseen skylight to converse with someone outside the confines of the church, and he'd fall into a bemused squint. A few silent seconds would tick, and then he'd smile broadly, raise the palms of his hands to the level of his chest, and spring into urgent action, sharing whatever luminosity he had managed to pull from his mind. This charming idiosyncrasy became a triumph of unconscious usefulness down the years in breaking apart anger and redirecting souls.

Because his preaching was never detached from his devotion to the Flesh and Blood of Christ, Tommy's homilies seemed both Eucharistic and enthusiastic. His piercing eyes, his intentionality, and the purposefulness of his words revealed a single-mindedness to direct souls to unshakable cohesiveness with God's will through divine revelation. He leaned on the uncompromising moral stances and incontrovertible teachings of the Church in order to shepherd his parishioners—and he did not care if they balked at his straightforwardness, fraternal correction, or clear disapproval of their sins. Wonderfully, as he exhorted his parishioners to fight for holier lives, the radiance of his heart-warming manner masked the severity of this request. His lone hope was to lead individuals to God's will for them, and through the narrow gate that swung open in the direction to heaven.

His constant goal was to unearth that missing *something* that lives in man's soul. He moved parishioners to grasp the divinity that lived within them because he grasped the mystery of the sacramental presence that moved him daily. He was famous for proclaiming in his booming voice: "People! If I can just get you to live every day with God and for God, then you'll know happiness and you'll be ready for whatever happens!" Parishioners have spoken of congregations falling into sustained silence in the aftermath of his homilies, as if they had been brought into private conversations between God and His Son.

"His homilies often left you spellbound. You'd find yourself hanging on every word, and sometimes the whole parish would just be sitting there in silence," said former parishioner Marybeth de Ribeaux. "It might have been tough teaching. He never hid anything, but it was done with so much joy. That's who he was, and he got away with it because you sensed that he valued your soul.

"There are few models who could ever have been better at radiating joy; John Paul II comes to mind. Fr. Wells exuded joy in a manner I'd never seen, and that's what he gave to the countless people who loved him. It was his enthusiasm for people that was so attractive to them — and clearly, he drove people closer to Jesus because of that. They saw his care for them as genuine. That's why he seemed to have thousands of friends. He knew Jesus and wanted to tell others about Him."

The Church's indissoluble truths lay deep in Tommy's soul, but he knew that until he articulately conveyed their sacred purposefulness, they could lie forever misunderstood and un-dervalued—so he revealed his own faith journey in homilies. He often threaded touching stories from his childhood into his preaching. He didn't hesitate to reveal embarrassing episodes from his teenage and college years, and he was brutally honest about often feeling powerless in overcoming his shortcomings and tendencies to sin. He wanted to convince his flock that although he was compromised by sin, the spotless teachings of the Church could never be. "His energy, enthusiasm, and love of Christ in preaching had parishioners thinking, 'Hey, he just really slapped me down, but he actually made it kind of fun,'" said Matt McDarby, a former parishioner. "There was nothing Pollyanna about him. He was as authentic as a priest can be. He spoke openly about his struggles, but he connected with people because he was able to connect theology and the day's readings to the listener's soul. He brought everything together—he brought the rich parishioners with the poor, the well-educated with the lesser educated, the holy with the not-so-holy. He just connected things. And it was because he led with joy."

He knew that his parishioners subconsciously begged for answers in their quest for truth—so he directed broken hearts and clouded minds toward the Holy Eucharist, knowing that its salvific significance needed to be at the root of that quest. His greatest homily, he knew, unfolded when he held high the Host at Mass. He would have preached on the Eucharist every day of his life. "When he held up the Host," Deacon Vita said, "everyone saw here was a priest in communion with that Host."

Carl Apgar, a scientist and former nonbeliever, converted because of Tommy's unconventional preaching style. "He held me completely captive. I was always a 'Thomas,' an enormous doubter who needed to see the nail holes, but he flipped everything on me," Apgar said. "He was able to take my clinical scientific skepticism and pile of doubts on the Eucharist—that I thought never could be figured out within my lifetime—and lead me to a fullness of faith and love of the Eucharist. He facilitated for me that the things unseen were more real than those seen with the eye. He made the unknowable knowable for me."

Apgar continued, "He spoke to save people's souls, and he spoke to save mine. He wanted to enter my soul and open it up, and even as a nonbeliever, I could see it from a thousand miles away. His gift was for changing people's lives. His homilies and 'way' seemed effortless. It had to be of God."

Tommy wanted to be a true shepherd and to shield his parishioners from wolves. He knew that poor preaching was a grave spiritual failing, and he held fast to St. Paul's words in Romans 10:14: "How can they believe in him of whom they have not heard? And how can they hear without someone to preach?" He offered catechesis both on an individual basis and in classrooms, but he may have executed it best within the joyful invitations laid out in his homilies, where he called listeners to conversion through the Magisterium and the words of martyrs, Church Doctors, and Jesus Christ Himself. His mission was the salvation of souls. So he used his gift for preaching as the warm glow of liberating truth to help lead all to heaven.

Fr. Rob Walsh, the chaplain of the University of Maryland's Catholic Student Center, said he was captivated by Tommy's preaching manner, even as a small child. He said he is a priest today because Tommy led him there.

"When he preached, he had this sleight-of-hand humor that you might see in a Pixar movie, where he would be speaking to two people at the same time. It was almost subliminal, next-level humor—where he'd say something startling that knocked you over with an awareness of your shortcomings, but do it with a smile on his face," Fr. Walsh said. "The key to Tom Wells was that his joy was transcendent, and that's why his preaching was wildfire. He offered an enthusiasm and joy that spread, and nothing could stop it.

"His preaching went well beyond his personality, charisma, or thoughts on the Catholic Faith. The joy in his preaching came from knowing that what he was telling his parishioners came from God. His life was joyful because he knew he was doing the will of the Father. He wouldn't have made sense to an atheist. Because he knew truth, he had an inner joy that the atheist wouldn't have been able to understand. So when he preached—whether it was a tough teaching or hard for some to hear—he had earned the trust of everyone in the church, and when a priest is able to do that, it's all over. Everything after is signed, sealed, and delivered."

"Priests are cast adrift today. So many seem to be speaking around things," Apgar said. "Fr. Wells hid nothing. He was never thwarted by speaking the truth. He wasn't thwarted by people's anger; he hit between the eyes and just kept coming—maybe you didn't get it and didn't get it and didn't get it. But he kept coming for you.

"He was speaking to save their souls. He was coming for their souls. This is how God loves."

13

Carpe Diem

On a pleasant summer morning in May 1979, a rawboned teen-ager named Doug stood on the side of Interstate 71 in rural Ohio with a banjo strapped to his arm; he was hitchhiking. Eager to become a bluegrass star at the Grand Ole Opry, young Doug had uprooted his life in a small Canadian town. He had just given his last seven dollars to the driver of his previous lift. He hadn't eaten a full meal in two days. So, when a stranger pulled over to pick him up, all Doug owned was his cherished musical instrument, the clothes on his back, and a desire for a sandwich.

Within a few minutes, the two men forged a bond. The driver had a fondness for what he considered the "humble way" of Canadians and the rugged beauty of their countryside. Doug felt immediately welcomed into the life of the stranger after recognizing the curious way in which he was able to get past pleasantries and penetrate quickly into his life with authenticity and easy joy. The man told Doug he was a priest, and soon there-after Doug admitted he hadn't stepped into a church in many years. For an unknown reason, the priest asked the hitchhiker if his parents were still regular Mass-goers. After answering in the negative, Doug saw a wave of disappointment spread over the priest's face.

"I was shocked [at his sorrow]. So I said, 'Why do you have to go to church? You can pray at home,'" Doug told him.

"To receive the Body of Christ," the priest bellowed, like the slam of a screen door in a hurricane. Thereafter, Doug remained wordless as the priest, with a depth of purpose Doug had never encountered, unfolded multilayered principles of the Mystical Body of Christ within its fountain of truth. The priest's presentation was as thrilling as it was illuminating; his verbal masterpiece drew from a peculiar palette of storytelling, unbridled wit, Scripture passages, and the deepest dogmas of the Faith, all expressed with the ease of a man adjusting the cuff of his shirt. But it was the priest's coolheaded self-assuredness in the truth of the Catholic Faith—and his obvious duty as a priest to proclaim it—that began to pull at Doug's conscience. As they drove on and conversed, Doug felt his soul being moved to long-forgotten light, as a moth draws near to a flame.

"I hadn't heard these things since third grade. Something came together," Doug said. "I knew that I had decided, right then and there, to return to the Body of Christ. That was the way back to recover what I had lost.... Somewhere in the depths of my preconscious mind, I was aware that this priest belonged to a world that I once knew. There was an interior joy and evident radiance that I had not encountered in anyone since my early days as a child. I wanted back into that world."

After a few hours of driving, the two prepared to part ways—the priest off to a seminary in Kentucky, and Doug set on building his music career in Nashville. The priest bought Doug lunch and handed him a twenty-dollar bill from his wallet. In thanksgiving and as repayment, Doug played some banjo tunes for him on the side of the road in Erlanger, Kentucky. He wrote down the priest's name and address on a road map and promised to stay in touch.

The roadside banjo concert was just Doug's first expression of his gratitude to the priest for leading him to recall the ultimate meaning of life. The young agnostic not only returned to his Faith, but he began to plunge into it. Years later, when Doug reemerged from an intense study of the Catholic Faith of his childhood, he had become the president of the Canadian Fellowship of Catholic Scholars. Today, Doug is a philosopher, theologian, deacon, prolific Catholic author, and married father. Just a single listen to one of his theologically layered podcasts brings one into an ocean of opulent Catholic thought.

Twenty-one years after the hitchhiking encounter, Doug Mc-Manaman traveled from his modest home in Canada to Bowie, Maryland, so he could properly mourn the death of the priest who gave him so much more than a lift, the murdered Msgr. Thomas Wells — Tommy.

"The joy I saw in Fr. Tom's eyes that day was living proof that what he was saying to me in that car was truth," Doug said. "I wanted what he had.... It was Fr. Tom's 'eye to eye' relationship, his genuine interest in this young person, his complete lack of pretense and his spirit of real joy — not the over-exuberance of [some priests], but the real joy — the subtle joy of having known the Lord and the love He has for us. I always wonder why I had to travel so far to encounter the right priest, the one who would inspire me to another life. There were so many priests around, so why another country, on a highway just outside of Columbus, Ohio?"

There was nothing drowsy or lackadaisical about Tommy's priesthood because he knew the clock ticked on it — and on his life. He regarded unannounced, unforeseen visits, like the one with Doug, as invaluable Christ-presented opportunities to invigorate and transform shriveled hearts. Accordingly, it was as if he always carried an unopened switchblade, ready to flick open at a moment's notice, to cut through human frailties, cynicism, ignorance, or false facades so that transformative light could be permitted to shine. He brought this radical carpe diem mentality into every corner of his priesthood and raised it to what eventually seemed an electric art form. The urgency to save souls was a wildfire within him—and he simply did not care whether his manner came across like a poem or a lightning strike. He just wanted to bring lonely souls into a place where they could sense Christ's presence, where they could see His gaze, where everything could forever be changed. He was on call, always.

So-called "random" encounters with Tommy would reveal to the unsuspecting that he possessed a startling form of interior joy. He'd made a decision early in his priesthood to crack himself open repeatedly in prayer so Jesus might pour His graces within him—and he, in turn, could enable whoever came across his path to receive those graces as well.

"Over and over, he captured people and brought them into the heart of things," said Margie Apgar, a former parishioner. "He had a way of leading you to joy. It was his power of knowing Christ and knowing and loving people that helped him lead people to places they didn't know."

David Russell, a Vietnam Marine Corps frontline soldier turned drifter, worked at a gas station down the road from Tommy's first parish, Sacred Heart. Tommy and the attendant began to strike up conversations at each fill-up. In the process of discovering the mental scars the war had inflicted on him, Tommy figured out that David was a Catholic. Their talks intensified—and within a year, the soldier became a daily communicant. Thereafter, Tommy asked him if he'd like to assist with youth catechesis, aware that his charred memories and feelings of exile might be buoyed by childlike innocence. The drifter obliged.

Sometime later, my uncle asked David if he'd consider the priesthood.

"I'm too old for the seminary," David replied. "Since it's August, it's too late to enter a program anyway."

"Not so fast," Tommy said. "Let's see what we can do."

Three weeks later, the Vietnam vet landed in a seminary. Fr. Russell has now been an ordained priest in the Washington, D.C., Archdiocese for more than three decades.

"He got me. He just had that way," said Fr. Russell, who preached at Tommy's memorial Mass on the eve of his funeral. "I felt as though a train with Tom on it had gone by—and as it passed, he'd stuck his hand out and grabbed me.

"I don't know how many priests got to ride on that train, but I do know many of us are priests today because of Tom Wells. His love of the priesthood, his joy for the priesthood—it came from his heart, and it came from our God. It wasn't just a way of life for Tom; it *was* his life."

Tommy regarded people as eternal souls, and whether they were known or unknown to him, he took artfully deep dives to try to bring them to divine light. Because he knew his interior inspirations were the voice of God, he saw them as opportunities—sudden plunges that God commanded him to take. So he "struck" in the medicine aisle of a drug store, in the confessional, at a Metro bus stop, at a Redskins game, in line at a Burger King, on a walk through a neighborhood. No manual, script, or time structure existed in these moments. But he believed that God had presented these opportunities, so he never minded engaging. He also understood that the Spirit accomplished the better part of his work anyway. Like the longing, pacing father of the prodigal son, Tommy was always anticipating someone's arrival, always ready to race out with Christ's message of measureless love. These abrupt encounters couldn't be measured on a human scale; they were urgent unions of souls. An untold number of individuals were affected by his plunging approach. If he sensed an atheist had a scintilla of desire to open his mind to know God, he sprang. If he suspected that someone wanted to break from communion with the Church, he sprang even faster.

"A good priest is always on the lookout for souls. He's less concerned about his own life, and thus less concerned about potential loss of revenues, the skill of his hired cook, or the quality and comfort level of the rectory and the needed renovations," Doug said. "Like Fr. Wells, good priests are more concerned for souls, the spiritual lives of the faithful; they want people to know that they're loved by God. And so a good priest will seize the moment; he'll notice it, recognize it for what it is. But many priests are not so orientated; the spiritual lives of the faithful are secondary, because their own spiritual lives are secondary."

One of the most lasting memories of my life came when a priest seized one of those "golden" moments. It unfolded in the span of about three minutes.

On a hot summer day a few years ago, an uncommon cancer, pleomorphic liposarcoma, had slunk into the brain stem of my relative Dave McGee and had finally managed to render him virtually powerless, confined to his hospital bed. The former athlete had fought for three years to lasso the bull-like cancer that shot all over his body. He knew that his leaving this world would leave his six young children fatherless.

So near the end, his wife, Maura (my cousin), and ten others packed into his small hospital room, hoping to comfort him as he lay dying. An unfamiliar priest sat at the foot of his bed, not saying much. Dave, fully alert to everything around him, attempted to join in as we spoke of the Orioles' many baseball failures, lopsided trades, and wrong-headed free-agent signings. We discussed family matters, the scalding summertime heat, the friendliness of the nurses, and the minutiae of our lives, but his powers of coherent speech had been mostly stolen.

We strained to understand Dave's words as they tumbled from his mouth, but we couldn't catch on. When he sensed our unease in making sense of his speech, he became quiet, and suddenly awkwardness spread into the devastation and sorrow. The room seemed to get sweatier with our tongue-tied grief. Maura just sat at the top of the bed, stroking the head of the only man she had ever loved. They had started dating early in high school. "Everything is fine, Dave," she let him know, "everything's fine." Dave remained quiet.

No one knew what else to do or say.

Then the door opened. A priest friend of the family stepped in. Over the years, his own spiritual and mental scars had become a source of blessing for those he served. He disregarded everyone but the dying man splayed out.

"Maura," he asked while moving toward Dave's bedside. "Can you give me some room?" Within moments of entering, he was inches from Dave's face.

This is what we saw.

"Dave," the priest said. "Listen. You're very near to Him now. And I know you might be afraid. But you can't be. Maura and the children will be taken care of. Everything will be fine with them."

Then he pulled a silver-dollar-sized pyx from his pocket.

"Hey, Dave, I'm gonna feed you now for the journey you're gonna take. Okay?" he said soothingly, pulling out a host, breaking off a piece smaller than a newborn's fingernail, and placing it on Dave's tongue. "Jesus Christ is within you now, Dave. And He's joining you for the journey you'll be taking to Him soon." This was startling to all of us visitors. None of us had chosen to step into this place.

"Soon, Dave, you're gonna see a light. Don't be afraid when you see it. I want you to walk toward it. I want you to run at it. And as you're running, Dave, you'll be called by name. A new name — but it's the name you've always had. You just haven't known it. But when you hear that name, you'll know right away that it's yours. Run when you hear your name. Run toward Him. It's Jesus who's calling you. That's where the warmth is. That's where He takes all this pain away."

Tears began to form in the corner of Dave's eyes. He couldn't speak in words; the single tear running down his cheek addressed all, saying what needed to be said: his eternal soul was brought to peace. Shortly thereafter, the former athlete died, perhaps departing with thoughts of sprinting Home.

Moments like this are carpe diem moments, when a priest takes a more profound and urgent dive while everyone else is saddled on the sidelines, anxiously twiddling their thumbs. Ephemeral platitudes — "I'll keep your family in my prayers and close to my heart" — gentle smiles, piety, or a turned-out psalm are functionless in this realm.

This priest who visited Dave was one of Tommy's closest friends. He, too, has distinguished himself for his reliance on the seize-the-day method of encountering souls — and his approach has become the compelling hallmark of his ministry. He understands that every instance is its own journey, so a daring vigilance accompanies his seizing action. Encounters often unfold without a moment's warning, but he takes the plunge every time because he knows his split-second decision to oblige or ignore the opportunity can make the ultimate difference for a soul. So today, thirty-plus years into his priesthood, he admits to only one goal as a priest: to pry open hearts to Jesus Christ and His message of salvation.

"It's what God expects of me. I'm a priest who serves souls," he said. "And He wants me going after every soul who is placed before me."

Msgr. Baker said that endless loops of the carpe diem moment are obtainable for all priests, and the most eager are permanently attuned to them. He says that a carpe diem approach is fundamental for his 145-plus future priests, especially in light of a growing sector of society that seems increasingly reluctant to buy into what they perceive as the Church's restrictions, rules, and rigidity. His seminary's vision statement echoes the idea of carpe diem: "We invite men to 'go up on the mountain' (Haggai 1:8) so that we might send down holy self-sacrificial shepherds for the people of God, to light a fire on the earth for the salvation of souls."

It's that very fire that sparks the carpe diem moment, but Msgr. Baker said that the spark simply cannot be lit if one of his future priests remains inattentive to the interconnectedness of the God-presented moment and his duty to address it *immediately*. Idleness or a spectator view today is unacceptable. Priests must take dives. The beguiling rector, whose dark-wood-paneled office is peppered with reminders of martyred saints, said that the ideal carpe diem priest cloaks himself in a magnanimous and humble manner, expressing at every moment his desire to step into a situation to help steer people toward Christ and the fullness of truth.

"We live in a society today that expects immediacy, so we really have to adapt to that," he said. "But addressing this immediacy cannot happen without first spending time in contemplation.

The Priests We Need to Save the Church

And it's through that that a priest becomes directed by God to attend to people with immediacy. The good priest is constantly attuned to God's will for him. He attempts to discern it always. It becomes almost natural for him — and very often, that includes the seize-the-day mentality. Often, in God's providence, when someone appears before him, the holy priest immediately engages the moment."

Msgr. Baker, Deacon McManaman, and some priests I spoke with worry that an all-too-common combination of worldliness, comfort, timidity, and lack of desire to engage souls has stunted some priests from sincerely attempting to lead individuals to an awareness of Christ, the Catholic Faith, and the state of their souls — no matter the time of day or situation. A few wondered if priests' lack of desire to engage souls was simply a case of not being able to give what they themselves do not have.

Another priest said the carpe diem moment dies if a priest neglects the demands of growing in his spiritual life: "Sadly, if a priest is not filled with a radiant joy and willingness to act, stemming from a deep prayer life and a profound relationship with the Holy Spirit, it would seem these transformative moments would rarely occur," he observed. "The soul in front of him must always be placed before his own. The priest concerned with the quality of that night's meals, his comfort, and the regular viewing of his favorite television show, will almost certainly be unable to recognize the carpe diem moment when it suddenly presents itself. It is a matter of orientation — everything must be focused on the salvation of the soul before him."

Jesus Christ, of course, is *the* model for the carpe diem priest. As God on earth, He created masterpieces of conversion that touched the deepest parts of souls, but as a human, Jesus also seemed practical-minded. He understood time constraints. And because He knew His time on earth was limited—and that He often wouldn't have the opportunity to encounter an individual again—He struck quickly. Each of His miracles, of course, are examples of His acting on the carpe diem moment—but perhaps His single greatest scriptural example of a "met" moment didn't involve the miraculous. It was His salvific encounter with the adulterous woman at the well. John's fascinating Gospel passage is the model that priests should follow in acting on the carpe diem moment. Jesus engaged in deliberate conversation. Seeing his intentionality, the woman responded. A lively back-and-forth began. In the process, Jesus sank the hook into her thirsting soul—and a cast-off sinner was converted. Within two days, most of the tiny Samaritan town of Sychar was converted as well—all because one man, God-made-flesh, took the time to raise one individual to a higher level of consciousness.

Much later, when Christ stooped to wash the dirty feet of twelve poor friends, this startling action overwhelmed them, especially Peter. Two millennia later, priests still mimic the audacity of that final act of humility. This is *the* model of the carpe diem dive, reaching souls with reckless displays of love.

Active, mission-based priests have always modeled themselves after Christ's mysterious movement of love. Their first rule of the carpe diem moment is to identify that it is, in fact, a moment of opportunity. The second rule is to discern quickly the contours of the moment, to call on the Holy Spirit, and then proceed to pour all of oneself into the encounter. After a priest enters into the moment, many say that a twofold action takes place: (1) a kenosis (self-emptying) envelops him to allow him to hear the Spirit's voice, and (2) after the Spirit's promptings are met, he's able to become a flame of charity that offers an invitation into a deeper reality.

The Priests We Need to Save the Church

Priest saints knew the carpe diem mentality well. It was as if they lived in an abiding state of warm invitation, where their every movement promoted what the apostle Philip cheerfully offered to Nathanael: "Come and see" (John 1:46). Their fundamental feature was their uninterrupted zeal to encounter folks and lead them to Christ. As bloodhounds for souls, they traveled to the darkest places—Christian-hating territories, war zones, communist nations—to dive straight into the hearts of strangers. They made themselves holy slaves to build up the household of heaven. They saw it as impulsive missionary work.

This type of spirit, spontaneity, and invitation is as vital as any single evangelistic tool the Church has at her disposal today. Whenever a priest encounters an unfamiliar soul, he should immediately recognize that he has just inherited a captive audience—and with today's social media–saturated universe, that's a big deal. It is within these precious moments of exclusive encounter that a priest should feel an urgency to stamp souls with indelible messages of Christ's love for them. He should feel an urge to attempt to reach the deepest place of the stranger's heart.

But for this mystical work even to begin (especially in these scandal-plagued days), the stranger must notice the priest's likeness to Christ, even if he's unable to name it outright, and must discern that at some level, the care that the priest provides goes deeper than a surface-level sociability. He must see the priest as one who esteems his soul. The stranger should feel as if he's in a rare sphere of caressing care throughout the entire encounter. It is this split-second, ad hoc decision to engage (a priest will either dive in or permit the moment to pass) that's able to stun souls into a move toward conversion. Hundreds of souls every day make the choice to explore and accept the Catholic Faith because of priests who decided to take this dive.

St. Philip Neri, considered one of the Church's most lovable and humorous saints, leaned into the spontaneous approach by frequently orchestrating one-day pilgrimages through the streets of Rome, where his joyful manner caught the attention countless numbers of onlookers. In what became known as "The Walk," happy bands of priests, seminarians, and their followers joined St. Philip with music, prayer, laughter, and camaraderie as they visited churches throughout Rome. They'd stop periodically to spread out blankets for picnics. Over the years, many thousands of onlookers, drawn by the exuberance of their glad-hearted devotions, joined with the merry pilgrimage and converted or re-converted to a life with Christ.

St. John Bosco was also a master of the spur-of-the-moment encounter. He'd gather poor but spirited boys for games, work-shops, conversations, and all-day outings to the Italian countryside on "Oratory Days," when the group immersed itself in the saint's benevolent manner and free-spiritedness. Thousands of boys es-tablished intense, lasting relationships with Christ due to this priest's happy-go-lucky yet reverent manner. "Run, jump, have all the fun you want at the right time," Bosco is famous for saying, "but, for heaven's sake, do not commit sin!"[35] As a young priest, St. John Paul the Great sensed the same power that freedom and vulnerability brought in extemporaneous moments. He frequently led college students and young adults to the hills and meadows of the Polish countryside, where the hikers enjoyed picnics and

---

[35] Quoted at "Salesian Youth Ministry," Salesians of St. Don Bosco, https://www.salesians.org.au/salesian-works/salesian-youth/74-youth-matters.

freely shared stories of their faith. These memories were cherished and often remembered in conversations by the pope.

The Acts of the Apostles, perhaps the most "active" book of the Bible, spills over with successful carpe diem moments. The story of Philip and the Ethiopian eunuch (Acts 8:26–40) is illustrative of one such moment that bore immediate fruit. Inspired by the Holy Spirit, Philip raced up to the chariot of the Ethiopian, who was providentially reading an Old Testament passage from Isaiah. Sensing Philip's zeal, the Ethiopian asked the stranger to interpret the passage for him. "Then Philip opened his mouth and, beginning with the scripture passage, he proclaimed Jesus to him." Overwhelmed by Philip's teaching, the Ethiopian requested to pull over his chariot in order that he could be baptized into the Faith. Then, in rather remarkable fashion, Philip departed from the man. But the eunuch went on his way "rejoicing," changed forever.

Later in Acts, Paul, alive in the Spirit after his conversion experience, relied on his courage and zeal to introduce Jesus' Resurrection in a land of idols. It was his opportunity to spread the gospel in Athens, a pagan city that teemed with statues and objects deifying foreign gods. Paul managed to arouse the curiosity of Athens' many philosophers, poets, and thinkers with his evangelization of Jesus in the town's synagogues. His words held enough conviction to earn him an invitation to orate on the peak of Mars Hill, or the Areopagus, an arena famous for its philosophical debates. Once there, Athens' greatest minds began to press Paul to share his thoughts on Jesus.

Rather than condemning their high-mindedness and pageantry of idols, Paul found the lone thread that linked them and then swiftly and cleverly used it to ingratiate himself to them and lead them to truth. "You Athenians, I see that in every respect you are very religious. For as I walked around and looked carefully at your shrines, I even discovered an altar inscribed, 'To an Unknown God,'" he said. After gaining their favor, the Spirit went to work through Paul: "What therefore you unknowingly worship, I proclaim to you" (Acts 17:22–23). He connected the dots directly to Jesus Christ. By keeping cool, creative, and true under the Mars Hill spotlight, he earned Christ's first Greek followers, Dionysius and Damaris and others, that day.

Two thousand years later, this same "common thread" approach is more important than ever in leading a secularly inclined society to the Catholic Faith. For Paul, it required attentiveness to the Spirit, keen insight, fast reaction time, and uncommon courage. On that hill stood a well-educated gathering of Greeks with high-minded, prideful philosophies and sharpened thought—and Paul knew he had his work cut out for him. He embraced the challenge, though, because he knew it was God who presented it.

Catherine de Hueck Doherty, the renowned foundress of the Madonna House Apostolate—known for its deep reverence and care for priests—was famous for challenging priests to take to the streets to show their love for mankind. She claimed that priests who simply walked their neighborhoods would ignite hope in its populace.

In her book *Dear Father: A Message of Love for Priests*, she relates the story of a Canadian Jesuit whose doctor asked him to take hour-long walks each day because he was feeling "run down." Fr. Keating intended to take strolls down the tidier, safer streets of Toronto, but Doherty urged him to walk the slums, especially down Cameron Street, which was an avenue of communists at that time. After some reluctance, he agreed. Initially, people hurled stones at him, and some of them hit him. He was mocked, and his priesthood was derided, but after some time, the neighborhood began to be converted and people were healed.[36]

"[Priests,] don't be afraid. Don't seek your 'identity.' You have it. You are a man touched by God and the laity know it," Doherty wrote. "We love you, even if some are hostile to you and castigate you. But don't be afraid. You have been touched by God and so it is not you who speaks, but he. Let us hear his voice, and because you allowed him to speak through you, we shall know him."[37]

---

[36] Catherine de Hueck Doherty, *Dear Father: A Message of Love for Priests* (Combermere, Ontario: Madonna House Publications, 1988), 193.

[37] Ibid.

Epilogue

My daughter Gabby and I were in the heart of a sixteen-hundred-mile college-visit road trip on the morning six men filed an eighty-page class action lawsuit against the Vatican and the USCCB for covering up "endemic, systematic, rampant and pervasive rape and sexual abuse."[38] As we traveled down lonely Southern roads — broken up by a visit to Elvis's humble shotgun-shack childhood home, Waffle House feasts, and long walks through old red-bricked-paved campuses — American bishops huddled in sullen, downtown Baltimore for their autumn 2018 plenary assembly. There, the Holy See would, at the last minute, slam shut what seemed an iron gate on the bishops' attempts to vote on measures designed to expose and tackle the Church's crisis of sex abuse and clergy homosexuality. A few days later, the bishops would *vote down* — by a nearly two-to-one margin — a proposal that urged the Vatican to release all documents related

---

[38] Catholic News Agency/EWTN, "Vatican, US Bishops Face Class-Action Lawsuit from Victims Of Clergy Sex Abuse," *Catholic World Report*, November 15, 2018, https://www.catholicworldreport.com/2018/11/15/vatican-us-bishops-face-class-action-lawsuit-from-victims-of-clergy-sex-abuse/.

to the numerous allegations of criminal activity against disgraced Theodore McCarrick.

It was announced that they'd get around to addressing Mc-Carrick's deplorable mess and the multiplicity of clerical vice the following February in Rome. Soon thereafter, though, on a plane trip home from World Youth Day in Panama, Pope Francis announced that expectations for measurable concrete action at the February meetings should be kept low. And just days before the summit's start, one of its pope-appointed organizers, Chicago's Cardinal Blase Cupich, confirmed that it would be unwise to "inflate expectations."[39] And just like that, a disillusioned and exasperated laity's high expectations for a reckoning of the moral chaos that had infiltrated the Church seemed to have been hijacked and then whitewashed by apathetic spiritual fathers. Indeed, throughout the three-day summit, questions about Mc-Carrick's meteoric rise to power while engaging in far-reaching and not-so-secret evil received continual deflection and virtual silence.

During a few of those long driving stretches in November, when country and bluegrass had lost its power to entertain, I drove to the music of silence as Gabby slept beside me. Within that quiet place, a thought slowly rose like a last sunrise that stretched into a mindful place within me—these four days on the road marked the last time we'd ever again be this close together. Gabby would be in college this time next year. Of course, I'd use this window of opportunity to offer Gabby what I hoped would

---

[39] Ed Condon, "What Can the Vatican Sex Abuse Summit Deliver?" Catholic News Agency, February 18, 2019, https://www.catholicnewsagency.com/news/analysis-what-can-the-vatican-sex-abuse-summit-deliver-69698.

be received as fatherly wisdom, but I knew that, at this point in our relationship, it could go unreceived. God had generously provided me with eighteen years to love and father her well. My time was all but up.

This book was written during a long wintertime in the Church, when much of America had come to regard the spotless, incorruptible Bride as a decaying organization beset by hidden evil—or at the very least a crippled Church of shattered credibility, torn away from her foundation. In speaking with many dozens of Catholic clergy and laity wearied by scandal throughout this past year, I found one issue rearing its head the most: the undisguised ascendency of fatherlessness within the Roman Catholic Church. As the fog of scandal pushed on, I began to see how the Church's hollowing out hadn't so much unfolded because of corruption, predation, or immoral carnality; it came because of overwhelming desertion—an anti-fatherhood had taken root in American parishes throughout the land.

To a man, each faithful priest who addressed the fog identified fatherlessness as the foundational reason for the stack of lawsuits, the spiritually drained and fallen-away Catholic laity, the subculture of grievous evil, shuttered parishes, and lamentable displays at the 2018 Youth Synod and USCCB fall gathering, as well as the February 2019 "clerical sex abuse summit." Given their nonaction at those events, bishops seemed not to comprehend that their moral integrity had mostly passed the point of no return. The absence of paternal shepherding and sacrifice for their flocks' eternal souls—which Ezekiel, Jeremiah, Paul, and our Savior Jesus Christ warned of—had set the frighteningly unholy table. As long as this anti-fatherhood persists as the Church's most tenacious weed, there will be no turning the corner in the Catholic Church.

The Priests We Need to Save the Church

So, with my writing of *The Priests We Need to Save the Church* completed and this naked image of fatherlessness on my mind, I thought of Gabby, my eldest child, lost to dreams beside me, and I addressed some of the dark-edged questions that often only silent thought can exhume. How had I done as a father? Where did I fail her, how often, and to what degree? Did small triumphs cohere, or disintegrate into impermanence? Could my love for Gabby be measured by its sacrificial dimension, or was it given lazily? Was I a man who truly fought for her, or just a guy who yielded? As her father, I held an impulse to shape her character and lead her to authentically lived Catholicity, but did my spiritual parenthood align with God's will, or just my own? The confluence of memory and conscience eventually brought me to the only question that mattered: Was I a father who had led my daughter to heaven? The categorical, correct answer will be given on Judgment Day.

I carried these considerations with me on a sun-splashed autumn Sunday morning at the University of South Carolina, where Gabby and I stepped out of our car and watched a logjam of college students walk down a narrow driveway for late-morning Mass at St. Thomas More Church. The kids hungered for some good news. The day before, their Gamecocks had blown a 17–0 lead in a stomach-punching loss to their SEC rival, the Florida Gators. Pre-Thanksgiving break exams lay directly ahead. The next three days forecast rain.

Then Fr. Marcin Zahuta, a former professional soccer player in his native Poland, stood for his homily and sparked what seemed Catholic fire.

"I have good news for everyone here today," he roared from behind a microphone-less ambo. "All of you are going to die." Then he smiled wide.

For the next fifteen minutes, I listened to the soul of an apostle shoveling up a cemetery of long-lost Catholic heirlooms, pointing students not to mediocrity, but to greatness. His robust words seemed like whirling flares pointing to the wilderness path of the saints; he touched on the reality of mortal sin, the cleansing work of purgatory, the Last Things, and the suffering each student was required to accept on his or her path to sanctity. He spoke of St. John Paul the Great's blood and then pulled out his own worn copy of St. Faustina Kowalska's *Diary: Divine Mercy in My Soul* and read an excerpt aloud, exhorting to his young congregation to look at the state of their own souls as they considered Jesus' words to the Polish mystic:

> Rest your head on My bosom and on My heart, and draw from it strength and power for these sufferings, because you will find neither relief, nor help, nor comfort anywhere else. Know that you will have much, much to suffer—but don't let this frighten you; I am with you. (no. 36)

After reading, he stood for a moment in silence, letting the students breathe in the meaning of Christ's tender words. He smiled his floodlight smile again. The life of Faustina and all the saints, he said in a commanding tone, required taking on a dimension of exacting pain to escape slavish behavior and attain the divine good—but accepting that pain was the remedy that would shape their souls and set them right for the throne of divine justice.

Marcin knew the Church existed to make saints. He was just a father showing them how.

He met with us next door after Mass at a bountiful spread at a Newman Center brunch, where FOCUS missionaries, students, adults, and neighbors amicably converged. After some time, he pulled us outside and led us down the path to pray with his newly acquired gem—a relic of St. John Paul II; he had recently built a small side chapel to house the treasure. His love for his home country's patron saint was inflamed. After expounding on the life of the hero of his youth, he transitioned to his own role at South Carolina, where he said his mission was to help college students grasp that sanctity, a life of virtue, and a hearty devotional life should be normal. He said that a primary duty of his spiritual fatherhood was to proclaim the Catholic Faith whole and inviolate. Anything less would cripple young souls, he said emphatically, and render his vocation impotent. He has tried to make the Newman Center a safe port against the battering winds of campus secularism and societal modernism. No one within his sight, he said, would be left a spiritual orphan.

"I can love [the college students] and love them and love them—but if I'm not their shepherd, then I've wasted my priesthood. If I don't fast for them, challenge them, catechize them, and lead them on the hard road to sainthood, then I'm just a hireling here," he said. "If I don't nourish the kids across the board with the truth of the Catholic Faith, then I'm a tragic failure as a priest. Notice that I used the word 'nourish' and not 'feed.' Too many priests are *feeding* their parishioners with unhealthy and false things or have just made the Church into a social justice network.

"The doors to my church are unlocked each hour of the day. The students need to know that, at 2:30 a.m., they can go to Christ before the tabernacle instead of somewhere else. We offer daily Adoration and frequent confessions so kids can get the sin out of their system. We pray the Rosary before daily Mass because these kids have come to know that they need to be nourished by Christ Himself. As a priest I am *in persona Christi capitis* [in the person of Christ the head]—and knowing that, I can't do anything but help purify these kids' souls; I can't be a part of the problem.

"There's a need for me to be bold and joyful because Jesus was bold and joyful," he continued. "Sure, I suffer because of my clear teaching sometimes, and a lot comes my way, but who cares? Jesus was rejected all the time. I should expect nothing less."

The risks Fr. Marcin takes to shepherd vigorously twenty-somethings into the rich patrimony of the Church's Tradition has paid off. In the spring 2018 semester, his parish experienced a 28 percent increase in parishioners from the previous year. When asked to explain the reason for the jump, he said he couldn't know with certainty, but he guessed that his presentation of the fullness of Catholic teaching, round-the-clock accessibility to the sacraments, and his push for personal sanctity all contributed. Daily confession was widely available for students. From time immemorial, mankind has desired simple, truthful solutions for the complexities of the soul. This priest offers them. He is the calm in the secular campus storm.

In another storm, in March 2019, 37 percent of Catholics told the Gallup polling agency that the recent news about sexual abuse of young people by priests had them personally questioning whether to remain Catholic, up from 22 percent in the aftermath of the scandals of 2002.[40] This book proposes something rather uncomplicated as a solution to a contemporary Catholic Church that often seems to be in terminal disarray: true spiritual father-hood, acting to create saints. Only faithful priests, through the

---

[40] Jeffrey M. Jones, "Many U.S. Catholic Question Their Member-ship amid Scandal," Gallup, March 13, 2019, https://news.gallup.com/poll/247571/catholics-question-membership-amid-scandal.aspx.

work of God, can raise this wreck. Modern, defective forms of spiritual fatherhood act in direct opposition to this goal, as the incriminating Gallup poll numbers show.

After spending the next few hours on a college tour led by a family friend, I steered our car west, feeling heartened about this one priest's supernatural faith and fatherly solicitude. Gabby, too, was caught off guard and moved by his priestly zeal, which fed our conversations as we traveled on. (And let's be honest: in my head I was thinking at the time, "Man, I hope she decides on Fr. Marcin—I mean South Carolina.")

Simply put, here was a man who wanted to become a saint. Better yet, perhaps, he was set on creating saints. In his ten-plus years as a college chaplain, Fr. Marcin had reached back into Catholic antiquity to shape the souls and consciences of his thousands of spiritual children. As an invasive faction within the modern Church has seemingly worked at de-emphasizing or even uprooting the teachings that point to the divinity of Christ, this bold and benevolent priest has chosen to expose the fountainhead of the Church's most sacred treasures. As the supernatural value of the sacraments, adherence to natural moral laws, reparation, penance, the saints, the daily Rosary, devoted prayer, ceremonial Catholic practices, and the pressing messages of Fatima, La Salette, and Akita have been choked out by Sunday pulpit amorphisms and whimsy, Fr. Marcin has created a groundswell of intentional young Catholics by heralding eternal divine law.

Fr. Walsh has managed the same at the University of Maryland, where's he has created one of the most dynamic Catholic student centers in America. In addition to helping to establish and support one of the nation's most effective Catholic pornography-healing ministries, the Fight Club, Fr. Walsh has helped to shepherd more than a dozen men into seminaries. During Fr. Shaffer's tenure as chaplain at George Washington University, his Newman Center more than doubled in size; he, too, has moved men into seminaries. Each priest opened up frontiers of the faith in the same buoyant, uncomprising manner of Sts. Philip Neri, John Bosco, and John Paul II. When a minister of God is joy-filled and strong, his children will be too. Shaffer and Walsh, who had been hand-led into the seminary by Tommy, have, in turn, led more than twenty men into the seminary.

Although I know there are many other such cassocked heroes besides these three college chaplains and the many other priests I've been privileged to speak with while writing this book, their presence today seems uncommon—and our uneasy culture and present evils witness to the lack of such fruit. It was my sincere effort in writing this book to uncover what priestly holiness looks like. Also included was an unearthing of my uncle, Msgr. Thomas Wells, to expose the lasting fruit that still matures because of his influence, and to identify those who are living examples of what his martyrdom sparked.

I imagine what the conversion of the world would resemble if there were a Tommy or a Fr. Marcin or a John Vianney in every parish. Rather than soft-pedaling the sacred teachings of the Faith, these priests have thrown open every door and window to proclaim them loudly. Many who have answered God's call to become other Christs have never had the privilege of encountering a priest like Tommy—and too many laypeople have never encountered priests who strive to shepherd their immortal souls to heaven, as Tommy once did.

As I look back at this past year and bring to mind the characteristics of the priests with whom I've spoken, I found twenty identifiers of a good priest. In closing, I offer them to you now.

The Priests We Need to Save the Church

Perhaps this priest who has these characteristics seems just a composite, but I know priests today who *are* this composite. They are the vessels God has employed to remedy the morally wounded Church. These Fathers are the heroic response. They represent the integrity of the priesthood. These identifiers mark their priesthood; they are the signatures of their sanctity, the stones of reconstruction.

Note: If you're a priest having arrived at this point, I encourage one action as you consider this list: do not resist it. Due to our fallen will and dyed-in-the-wool tendency to reject instinctively that which we do not do, be ruthless with yourself as you consider each identifier. Rather than pushing two or three or even the majority of characteristics away, I beg you to take them before the Blessed Sacrament, with a searching eye and an openness to the Spirit. (This, of course, goes for seminarians, laity, and all religious as well).

1. He keeps the Blessed Sacrament in a small chapel near his rectory bedroom to keep him company when he grows lonesome and weary.

2. He has crucified himself to worldly charms and lazy habits.

3. He often walks through his neighborhood, praying the Rosary.

4. His patron saints come to mind at various points of the day, heartening him.

5. The ringer on his cell phone, which rests on his nightstand, remains on while he sleeps, as he anticipates emergencies.

6. He prays the Divine Office with reverence and intentionality, knowing that it calibrates his soul and the solemn manner in which he celebrates a liturgically beautiful Mass.

7. He has manly intentionality; he has banished fear from his life (other than of God) as he strives to meet his full potential.

8. His servitude includes devoting a daily Holy Hour, offered for an individual member of his parish.

9. He daily reads a few pages of a spiritual masterpiece or from a Church Doctor, continually striving to become a reservoir of wisdom and grace for his flock.

10. He celebrates Mass each day, including his "days off" whenever possible, and offers to celebrate private Masses at suffering parishioners' homes.

11. He examines the state of his priesthood daily, discerns when small corruptions might be settling in, and fights them off as if they were Satan.

12. He favors the narrow path, consenting to a form of asceticism each day.

13. His motto for preaching is framed by Pope St. Pius X: "When you teach in church you must not seek for the applause of the crowd but that they should weep: the tears of your listeners should be your praise."

14. His daily toil and corporal works intensify and expand when he considers his duty to his heavenly Mother.

15. His center of gravity is the Eucharistic Face of Christ, where his priesthood is absorbed into its mystery.

16. He spends a few quiet moments each day mentally resting against Jesus' beating heart, like St. John.

17. He's an apostolic man attuned to souls, constantly guarding them against evil.

18. He's devoted to a life of burning interior prayer, aware that this is where graces are obtained, and where his ministry is fueled.

19. His habits of virtue are firm; as Christ is holy, he strives to help his parishioners to become holy.
20. He has built his entire priesthood on a childlike dependence on God.

This is the priest we need to save the Church.

About the Author

Kevin Wells is a former Major League Baseball writer, award-winning journalist, and author of *Burst: A Story of God's Grace When Life Falls Apart*. He is a freelance writer and an active evangelist who speaks on various Catholic topics. He is president of the Monsignor Thomas Wells Society for Vocations, which financially and prayerfully commits itself to the promotion of strong priests and seminarians and to the practice of the fullness of the Catholic Faith. Kevin's work with youth earned him the James Cardinal Hickey National Figure Award from the Archdiocese of Washington, D.C. Kevin lives in Millersville, Maryland, with his wife and three children. He loves baseball, reading, and his backyard fire pit (with many men gathered around).

If you would like to obtain Msgr. Wells's book, *From the Pastor's Desk: Spiritual Reflections*, or learn more about Msgr. Wells or the Msgr. Thomas Wells Society, please visit the Msgr. Thomas Wells Society Facebook page or visit KevinWells.org.

Sophia Institute

Sophia Institute is a nonprofit institution that seeks to nurture the spiritual, moral, and cultural life of souls and to spread the Gospel of Christ in conformity with the authentic teachings of the Roman Catholic Church.

Sophia Institute Press fulfills this mission by offering translations, reprints, and new publications that afford readers a rich source of the enduring wisdom of mankind.

Sophia Institute also operates the popular online resource CatholicExchange.com. *Catholic Exchange* provides world news from a Catholic perspective as well as daily devotionals and articles that will help readers to grow in holiness and live a life consistent with the teachings of the Church.

In 2013, Sophia Institute launched Sophia Institute for Teachers to renew and rebuild Catholic culture through service to Catholic education. With the goal of nurturing the spiritual, moral, and cultural life of souls, and an abiding respect for the role and work of teachers, we strive to provide materials and programs that are at once enlightening to the mind and ennobling to the heart; faithful and complete, as well as useful and practical.

Sophia Institute gratefully recognizes the Solidarity Association for preserving and encouraging the growth of our apostolate over the course of many years. Without their generous and timely support, this book would not be in your hands.

www.SophiaInstitute.com
www.CatholicExchange.com
www.SophiaInstituteforTeachers.org

Sophia Institute Press® is a registered trademark of Sophia Institute.
Sophia Institute is a tax-exempt institution as defined by the
Internal Revenue Code, Section 501(c)(3). Tax ID 22-2548708.